180 DEVOTIONS

~ for When ~
Life Is Overwhelming

Hilary Bernstein

BARBOUR
PUBLISHING

Print ISBN 978-1-63609-368-0

Published by Barbour Publishing, Inc., 1810 Barbour Drive, Uhrichsville, Ohio 44683, www.barbourbooks.com

Our mission is to inspire the world with the life-changing message of the Bible.

Printed in the United States of America.

INTRODUCTION

Did you know that *whelm* is a word? *Whelm*, in fact, means to turn upside down, immerse, engulf, or submerge. Many days you might end up feeling whelmed. Things in life get all topsy-turvy and start to feel a little out of control.

Once you understand what it means to be whelmed, what does it mean to be overwhelmed? *Overwhelm* means you're overcome by superior force; you're overpowered in thought and feeling; or you're covered over or engulfed completely.

Overwhelm seems like an expected part of life today. Almost every woman describes herself as feeling overwhelmed in some way. The reasons are as different as the women, but the undeniable fact is we're living in an age of overwhelm.

If we really are living in an age of feeling overpowered, overcome, and completely submerged, how can the Lord help? What does His Word say about our situation? These devotions will help you process your overwhelming thoughts with the truth of the living God. May He use them in a powerful way to bring His peace and calm to your life!

UNCHANGING

*"Even to your old age I will be the same, and even to
your graying years I will carry you! I have done it, and I
will bear you; and I will carry you and I will save you."*

ISAIAH 46:4 NASB

Overwhelm can look like a million different things
throughout your life: Classes and grades when you're a
student. Relationship choices when you're single. Com-
munication and intimacy issues when you're married.
Infertility or pregnancy concerns, then discipline and
developmental struggles as parents. Overwhelm can look
like caring for aging parents, balancing jobs and homes and
relationships. Uncertainty in current events and finances
and leadership might feel too overwhelming. Health issues
affect everything, and decision fatigue weighs heavily.

Yet, in the middle of all that weighs you down, the
Lord always is the same. He will save you. He will lead
you every day, whether you realize it or not. And He will
carry you from your youth to your old age. When everything else in your life seems to change with surprise and
uncertainty, the Lord won't change. He's stable and steady.
He has promised to carry you through it all.

---

*Father, I praise You for Your unchanging ways.
Thank You for Your love and provision and protection.
Thank You for carrying me all throughout my life.*

POPULARITY CONTEST

*"Enter through the narrow gate. For wide is the gate
and broad is the road that leads to destruction, and
many enter through it. But small is the gate and narrow
the road that leads to life, and only a few find it."*

MATTHEW 7:13–14 NIV

The choices of a believer of Christ should look very different from the choices the world encourages. Is this kind of life popular? No. And even women with the toughest skin may get discouraged when they feel out of place.

Think about how Jesus lived. He clearly was different. And consider His teachings. He didn't shy away from the fact that experiencing forever life isn't for everyone. In fact, the way is so narrow only a few find it. That kind of road is one that most people choose *not* to travel.

If you try to please the world with a popular way of living, you'll miss what the Lord prefers. But when you choose to follow His narrow, unpopular way, you'll end up with a reward much greater than anything this world offers.

---

*Lord, You never promised that following You would
be easy. In fact, because Your gate is small and Your
road is narrow, I know I can't choose what the world
approves. I want to please and worship only You.*

DISTRACTED

We are no longer to be children, tossed here and there
by waves and carried about by every wind of doctrine, by
the trickery of people, by craftiness in deceitful scheming;
but speaking the truth in love, we are to grow up in all
aspects into Him who is the head, that is, Christ.

EPHESIANS 4:14–15 NASB

If you pay much attention to the news, overwhelm has an uncanny way of rushing in like a tidal wave. Do you feel like you're carried about and tossed here and there by current events? Does the daily news alarm and distract? The media manipulates. People trick and scheme with deceit. Even so, what will you do?

The apostle Paul gave fantastic advice in Ephesians: speak the truth in love and grow up in all aspects into Christ. That means that you can shut out all the chaos and noise of this world, even when you're in the middle of it. Don't be afraid to speak the truth in love. Instead of worrying or overthinking things, concentrate on growing up in all aspects into Christ. When He becomes your focus, you'll be strong, steady, and rooted in truth.

Lord Jesus, I'm so thankful I don't have to worry about
the always changing problems of this world. I want to
grow up in all aspects into You. Please guide me!

HE'S THE ONE

*O LORD, how many are my foes! Many are rising
against me; many are saying of my soul, "There is no
salvation for him in God." But you, O LORD, are a shield
about me, my glory, and the lifter of my head. I cried aloud
to the LORD, and he answered me from his holy hill.*

PSALM 3:1–4 ESV

Life is messy, in part, because people are messy and relationships are messy. Betrayal and mockery are just a couple
of the heartbreaking effects of the messiness; as hard as
they are to endure, they're almost an inevitable part of life
in this fallen, sin-stained world.

Even with disappointment and heartache, there's
still hope. Despite the hurtful things that happen in this
life, who is the Lord? He's a protective shield around
you. He's your glory. He's the lifter of your head. In the
middle of your heartache and tears, He's the One to lift
you up in protection and love. He's the One to mend
your brokenness.

---

*Lord, when it seems my life is filled with despair and
brokenness, I'm thankful I always can turn to You. No
matter what, You are there as my comfort and protection.
You are the Lifter of my head even in my darkest days.*

WHO WILL YOU PLEASE?

*Just as we have been approved by God to be entrusted
with the gospel, so we speak, not intending to please
people, but to please God, who examines our hearts.*

1 THESSALONIANS 2:4 NASB

People pleasing is exhausting. Not only are most people
opinionated, but they also are fickle and change their minds
when you least expect it. When you try to go through life
living up to everyone else's expectations and whims, you'll
wear yourself out in a hurry.

But what if people pleasing wasn't part of your life?
What if, instead of caring about what others thought,
you chose to please God? God is the One who knows
you better than anyone else. He created you! God is the
One who chose to entrust you with the Gospel. You didn't
have to do anything on your own; He approved *you*. And
God is the One who examines your heart—no one else.
Because of that, He's the One and *only One* you should
be concerned about pleasing.

---

*Lord God, I'm amazed that You chose me. And You've
approved me to be entrusted with Your Gospel! Please
help me focus on pleasing You and You alone.*

TURNING YOUR HEART

*Turn my heart toward your statutes
and not toward selfish gain.*
PSALM 119:36 NIV

Like it or not, it's so easy to get distracted and tempted by selfish gain. If you think you can get ahead and prosper in a certain area—whether it's financially, professionally, or even socially—you might get sucked into spending a lot of time and energy trying to make things happen. You want to do well. You want to see yourself succeed. It's tempting to think that having something in particular could fulfill your desires. But if you focus on getting ahead, you might fail to see all the good that could be done right now.

The psalmist gave wise advice in Psalm 119:36. Instead of praying for better things and focusing on selfish gain, pray that the Lord would turn your heart toward His statutes. How would life look if you turned your heart and your thoughts toward His Word? How could your focus change if you chased after His truth instead of being overwhelmed by the passing fancies of this world? How radically does God Almighty need to turn your heart?

---

*Father, please turn my heart toward the truth in Your
Word. I don't want to be distracted by this world.*

ALWAYS FULL

*Out of his fullness we have all received grace
in place of grace already given.*
JOHN 1:16 NIV

As you spend your days giving your attention to others, it's natural to feel empty, like you have nothing more to give. If you were like a bathtub—filled to the brim with water each day—by the end of a busy, overwhelming day, most of your water would be drained out. That's simply part of a life with limits. Humans don't have unending resources of energy. We all have just twenty-four hours in a day.

But praise the Lord that He is a God without limits! He doesn't get tired or overwhelmed. His energy and strength don't drain away. He's always full. Out of His fullness, He lavishes you with grace upon grace. He gives you grace; then He heaps on more. When you're feeling depleted, turn to Him. Ask Him to reveal His grace to you in a new way today.

*Thank You, Father, for Your good gift of grace!
When I feel so empty, I'm thankful You share
Your grace with me out of Your fullness.*

FAITHFULLY FILLED

But this I call to mind, and therefore I have hope:
The steadfast love of the LORD never ceases; his
mercies never come to an end; they are new
every morning; great is your faithfulness.
LAMENTATIONS 3:21–23 ESV

When life becomes a blur of busyness and the weight of overwhelm presses down like a heavy burden, it's easy to focus on the urgent. Yet instead of only tending to the tasks, thoughts, and emotions that scream for your attention, you can choose to think of other things. You can choose to call truth to mind and be filled with hope in the process.

What's the truth that deserves your focus? The Lord's love never changes and never ends. His mercies never end either. In great faithfulness and love, the Lord lavishes you with new mercies every single day. Instead of feeling like you're running on empty, you can experience absolute fullness faithfully poured out by the Lord.

Father, You're so faithful and kind! Your steadfast
love never ceases. Your mercies never end. I praise
You for how very great Your faithfulness is.

WHAT'S SO GOOD ABOUT SUFFERING?

In all this you greatly rejoice, though now for a little
while you may have had to suffer grief in all kinds of
trials. These have come so that the proven genuineness
of your faith—of greater worth than gold, which
perishes even though refined by fire—may result in
praise, glory and honor when Jesus Christ is revealed.

1 PETER 1:6–7 NIV

At its very core, suffering is not enjoyable. Pain, distress, and loss aren't experiences most people want to endure, let alone find reason to rejoice in. But in a believer's life, suffering and endurance have the potential to grow into something beautiful.

Grief and suffering have a unique way of proving how genuine your faith is. Do you have faith at all, or are you swept away by bitter feelings and hurt? All your endurance ends up strengthening you too. Like hard work brings good results, so can suffering and endurance.

What are some of the spiritual benefits found in hard times? You'll be able to rejoice and praise the Lord, as well as glorify and honor Him. Rejoicing in the middle of suffering and praising in the middle of endurance are some remarkable gifts!

Lord, You can bring beauty out of ashes. You
can bring peace and joy out of pain. Thank You
for the way You work wonders in my life!

DOING GOOD

*Therefore, as we have opportunity, let us do
good to all people, especially to those who
belong to the family of believers.*

GALATIANS 6:10 NIV

Have you ever looked around at your circumstances and realized that the Lord has brought everything together in an amazing way? You might try and try to orchestrate something; but when God's hand is at work, it's undeniable—things happen.

When you notice He's working and bringing things together in an incredible way, don't let the moment pass. Do something! When you see that He has presented an opportunity, do good to all people. When you think of a way to help someone else, do it! When the Lord gives you an idea of how to improve someone's life or situation, act on that thought. Be a doer instead of only having good intentions.

As you begin to do more for others, you'll start thinking of more good things to do. It's a lot like a snowball that gets bigger and bigger. Keep doing good to all people, especially other believers!

---

*Father, please help me see the opportunities
You bring my way. And please help me be
more like You by doing good to all people!*

FINDING THE WAY

*Through love and faithfulness sin is atoned for;
through the fear of the LORD evil is avoided.*

PROVERBS 16:6 NIV

Bad things happen. While unfortunate events might be the last thing you want or deserve, they're consequences of the fall. The good news is you don't have to get stuck dwelling on the bad things that happen.

The even better news? Jesus came to this earth to offer forgiveness to all who believe in Him and call on His name. That means if bad choices have been a regular part of your life, you don't need to feel stuck. There's a way out, and that way is the Way, the Truth, and the Life. All you need to do is ask Him for His help.

It's Jesus' love and faithfulness that make you right despite your sins. And when you recognize Him for who He is, you'll begin fearing Him with honor and respect. As a result, your life choices will reflect your beliefs. You'll avoid sin as you choose to live for Him.

Lord Jesus, I am so thankful You are the way out of all the mistakes and mayhem of this life. Thank You for Your love and faithfulness. Thank You for taking care of my sins for me. I believe in You and want to live for You!

DIFFERENT

*"Behold, I am sending you out as sheep in the midst of
wolves, so be wise as serpents and innocent as doves."*
MATTHEW 10:16 ESV

While it might seem obvious, there should be a stark
difference between believers and nonbelievers. Like light
and darkness are different, so is someone who trusts in
Christ and someone who doesn't. Believing in Christ and
accepting His teaching and ways make you different. It
separates you from those who choose not to accept Him.

Because you're decidedly different, it's important to
live like it. Try to use wisdom in the things you think, say,
and do. As you do, you'll live like you're set apart for Christ.
This may mean you're different from the people you spend
most of your time with, but that's okay. Living a different
life simply means you're honoring Christ in your choices.
As His follower, that's how you honor and thank Him.

---

*Lord Jesus, it can be so tempting to set my attention on
things of this world, whether it's pleasures or possessions,
relationships or status. I want my life to reflect my
relationship with You. Please help me be wise and innocent,
two things that seem so uncommon in the world today.*

RIGHT VS. WRONG ANGER

BE ANGRY, AND YET DO NOT SIN; do not let the sun go down on your anger, and do not give the devil an opportunity.
EPHESIANS 4:26–27 NASB

One common misconception about anger is that it's a bad thing. But when anger doesn't turn into aggression or wrath, it's simply an emotion you can expect to experience. The key to experiencing anger, though, is not falling into sin because of your anger.

How can you be angry without sinning? The apostle Paul gave some practical advice: don't fixate on your anger. His suggestion is to not let the sun go down on your anger. When you dwell on all that makes you feel angry, your angry thoughts and feelings have a way of multiplying and affecting all aspects of your life. Sometimes it might even feel good to stay angry and let your negative feelings change the way you look at everything. Resist this temptation! Don't let anger take root. Experience it, deal with those angry feelings, and choose to move on.

Father, sometimes I don't know what to do with my emotions. You've created me as an emotional being, though. Please help me realize I can feel angry. But please also help me not sin because of anger.

CANCEL THE PERFORMANCE

*His pleasure is not in the strength of the horse, nor his
delight in the legs of the warrior; the LORD delights in those
who fear him, who put their hope in his unfailing love.*

PSALM 147:10–11 NIV

In today's outward-obsessed culture, it's easy to fall into
the trap of thinking that performances matter. But does it
matter how much you achieve? Does it truly matter what
you look like? Of course not!

Outward appearances are deceiving, and no one
knows that better than the Lord of all. God sees into the
heart of every human, and He doesn't take pleasure or
delight in strong bodies or achievements that thrill the
masses. What He delights in is a heart that fears Him.
He finds great pleasure when you choose to put your hope
in Him and His unfailing love.

Instead of getting so wrapped up in keeping busy,
let yourself get consumed by the awe of your heavenly
Father. Worship and praise Him. Honor and revere His
name. Put your complete hope in Him. That's what truly
matters.

---

*Lord, it's so easy to get caught up with things
I can see. And even when I don't like it, I think
about what others think. Please help free me from
pleasing anyone but You. I want to put all my hope
and trust in You—not in my own strength or abilities.*

TOO MUCH

But godliness with contentment is great gain,
for we brought nothing into the world, and we
cannot take anything out of the world.

1 TIMOTHY 6:6–7 ESV

Isn't it funny that too much really is too much? When it comes to stuff, having too much really is too much. No matter how you acquire your possessions, it takes a lot of time and energy to care for your belongings. And when you need to get rid of what you don't want or need, downsizing takes an enormous amount of time and energy.

Belongings don't fill our lives with joy and contentment like we think they should. Once the sparkle and shine of something new wears off, we're left with the maintenance. Plus, all those material possessions won't last forever. We come into and leave this world without a thing.

What would your life look like if, instead of investing your time and money into acquiring things that are bigger and better, you chose to be thankful for exactly what you have? What if you began to truly feel content with the gifts the Lord has given you?

Father, please forgive me for placing such importance on stuff. Please help me not get so caught up in the things of this world. Instead, I want to be grateful for each blessing You've given me out of Your kindness and love.

NEVER ALONE

You have held my eyelids open;
I am so troubled that I cannot speak.

PSALM 77:4 NASB

When life's hurts and troubles pile up and feel like walls that are closing in, the sadness, grief, and disappointment bring you to your knees. While you're there, knowing you can't go on in your own strength, turn to the Author and Perfecter of your faith. His power is perfected in your weakness.

You may not be able to go on, but He can and will. The Lord will hold your eyelids open. He will wipe away your tears and collect them in a bottle. He sees and hears and knows all you're facing. And He's there for you, offering comfort and peace that can't be explained. As you cry to Him for mercy, expect Him to move and work in your life. He is for you, even in the middle of your darkest days and nights. When you need to endure, He's walking beside you so you're never alone.

Lord Jesus, facing troubles never is easy. Endurance isn't enjoyable either. Thank You for never leaving me, no matter what I go through. Please give me Your strength in my weakness. I want to turn to You with all my disappointment and despair. No matter what happens in this life, I trust You.

FAITH? OR FEAR?

And He got up and rebuked the wind and said to
the sea, "Hush, be still." And the wind died down
and it became perfectly calm. And He said to them,
"Why are you afraid? Do you still have no faith?"
MARK 4:39–40 NASB

When you find yourself in a surprising situation and you react in fear, you might look back in hindsight and wonder why you were ever afraid. You're not alone. Jesus spent years pouring into His disciples' lives, and fear still was a natural reaction for them. In fact, they were so fearful that a storm would wipe out their boat that they woke Jesus from His sleep to ask for help.

Like Jesus' disciples, you can approach Him at any time to ask for help. And like Jesus' disciples, you can trust Him in faith. You don't have to fear. Instead of feeling overwhelmed by fearful, anxious thoughts and concerns, know the One you're trusting and leave matters with Him.

Lord Jesus, You're amazing. You can calm the wildest seas,
and You can calm the storms that rage around me. I want
to trust You and be filled with faith. Please ease my fears.

WHO GETS TO CELEBRATE?

*When pride comes, then comes disgrace,
but with humility comes wisdom.*
PROVERBS 11:2 NIV

Pride is so ugly. When you think highly of yourself, there's a good chance that you're thinking of yourself more highly than you should; and eventually you'll become much more important or significant in your own eyes than you actually are. The scary thing about pride is that it can creep up on you in ways that you don't recognize right away. And if you refuse to deal with it? You can be sure that at some point, maybe when you least expect it, disgrace will come.

If you want to avoid pride, choose a life of humility. By not thinking of yourself more highly than you should or by choosing to value others like you value yourself, you'll experience blessings that come from a life of wisdom. Choosing pride might seem so much easier than choosing humility. But when you choose pride, you'll be the only one enjoying your own celebration of your puffed-up self. When you choose humility, you shine the spotlight on others so *they* get to celebrate.

Father, I don't want to be proud. I know it's easy to puff myself up. Please help me remember who I am and who You are. Please help me live a humble life.

SETTING YOUR HOPE

Therefore, preparing your minds for action, and being sober-minded, set your hope fully on the grace that will be brought to you at the revelation of Jesus Christ.

1 PETER 1:13 ESV

What triggers your feelings of overwhelm? A lack of preparation might often be to blame. If you're caught by surprise or are unprepared, you end up feeling like you've fallen behind and you may not have any idea how to catch up.

You may not get a chance to fully prepare for all of life's situations, but you can prepare your mind. The apostle Peter explained how you can prepare your mind for action: Keep yourself alert. Instead of choosing evil desires, obey the Lord. Instead of flitting from thing to thing or thought to thought, be sober-minded. Knowing that Jesus is the One who gives you grace to live this life, set your hope completely in Him for the life that's yet to come. Embracing that reality is a fantastic way to prepare your mind.

Lord Jesus, thank You for Your grace! I put all my hope in You alone. Please help me prepare my heart and mind for the things I'll encounter in this life.

YOUR GOOD WORK

For I am confident of this very thing, that
He who began a good work among you will
complete it by the day of Christ Jesus.

PHILIPPIANS 1:6 NASB

When you're in the middle of the busyness of life, keeping the big picture in mind can be tricky. Day-to-day demands distract you from what really matters.

Yet even if you lose sight of the big picture, the Lord never does. According to Ephesians 2:10, you were created in Christ Jesus for good works that God prepared in advance. He started that good work in you, and just as He knows ahead of time what you're meant to do, He'll complete it in you too. Life may have a sneaky way of shifting your focus from what truly matters, but remember that God is doing something really good through you. Even if you don't see His big picture in the tiny moments of your life, He knows what He's doing. And someday, He'll complete that good work in you.

Father, some days I can't seem to see the glimpses of the
good work You're doing in and through me. Please help
me trust You and follow Your lead. I don't want to get
in the way of the good work You've planned for me!

JUST KEEP SWIMMING

Deep calls to deep in the roar of your waterfalls;
all your waves and breakers have swept over me.
By day the LORD directs his love, at night his song
is with me—a prayer to the God of my life.

PSALM 42:7–8 NIV

Imagine your life of faith as yourself stepping out into a large body of water. Eventually you'll walk so far out that your feet won't touch the bottom anymore. You'll need to swim, regardless of whether the waters are calm or choppy. Waves and breakers will sweep over you. The rush and roar of the water will seem deafening.

As you tread water in those parts of life when you're so very far from the safe and sure shore, keep swimming. Forget about the feeling of the land under your feet. As you let the waves wash over you, remember you're not alone. The Lord won't let you drown. Day and night, He'll direct you in His love.

As you venture far out into your life of faith, you'll never be sure where He'll take you. But you can know He'll lovingly take you to amazing places for His good purposes. Just keep swimming!

Father, as much as I'd like a safe journey, I'm ready and willing to be used by You. Take me where You want me to go. Please help me boldly follow You by faith. Even when my feet can't touch the bottom, please help me keep trusting You.

PLEAD FOR WORKERS

*Then He said to His disciples, "The harvest is plentiful,
but the workers are few. Therefore, plead with the Lord
of the harvest to send out workers into His harvest."*

MATTHEW 9:37–38 NASB

Every day you see the Pareto Principle at work: 20 percent
of the people do 80 percent of the work. If you're one
who's keeping busy with 80 percent of the work, hopefully you're feeling fulfilled by the work you do, even if
it's sometimes tiring.

As humans, we're not meant to live life or attempt
ministry on our own. And even if the Pareto Principle
happens often, it shouldn't be used as an excuse to not
work and to just assume others will do what's necessary.

Work is an intended part of life. Just as physical
labor is necessary, spiritual work for the kingdom of
God is necessary too. Jesus knows there's plenty of work
to be done for His kingdom, and He also knows there's
always a need for more workers.

If you're not serving the Lord in some way, get
working! Find a way to share the love of Jesus with others.
And if you're already working hard, pray and plead with
Him to send more workers to help you.

---

*Father, please send more workers into Your
harvest. May we work hard for Your glory.*

BITE YOUR TONGUE

*Do not let any unwholesome talk come out of your mouths,
but only what is helpful for building others up according
to their needs, that it may benefit those who listen.*

EPHESIANS 4:29 NIV

Though you may often hear the reminder to think before you speak, that's often easier said than done. Blurting out reactions before really thinking about your words is so easy. But as natural as it might seem, it doesn't mean it's the right thing to do.

The Bible challenges believers to say things that are helpful to listeners at all times—not only when you're in a good mood or all seems right in the world. When you're frustrated and feel like you want to say whatever's on your mind, don't. If you know you shouldn't say something, bite your tongue. Don't let corrupting words come out of your mouth. It would be better to say nothing at all than to say something bad.

And what would be better yet? Words that build people up. Words that benefit listening ears. Words that make lives better.

---

*Father, it's tough to watch my tongue and control my
words! The good news is it's not impossible! Please help
me consider the words I use before I say them.*

WHEN I CALL

*Answer me when I call to you, my righteous
God. Give me relief from my distress; have
mercy on me and hear my prayer.*

PSALM 4:1 NIV

When you need help, you don't want to wait around.
You want to get help right away! Just like you ask people
around you to help with some emergency, you can ask
the Lord too.

When you feel overwhelmed, tell Him! When you're
upset or confused, let Him know and ask for help! If anyone can help, it's the Lord of hosts. He can relieve you
from your distress. He will hear your prayer and answer
you with mercy and grace.

Instead of trying to take matters into your own hands
and carry all your burdens alone, share them with the
One who created and cares for you. Share your concerns
with the Lover of your soul. When you call to Him, He
will answer.

*My righteous God, I'm so grateful I can come
to You! Please give me relief from my worries.
Please have mercy on me and hear my prayer.*

STRONGER IN THE LONG RUN

*Consider it all joy, my brothers and sisters, when
you encounter various trials, knowing that the
testing of your faith produces endurance. And let
endurance have its perfect result, so that you may
be perfect and complete, lacking in nothing.*

JAMES 1:2–4 NASB

Has the prospect of suffering ever excited you? Does growing in endurance bring a smile to your face? Unless you're unlike most people in the world, facing hard times isn't enjoyable.

Although you may not be excited to face your next trial, James taught that believers should find joy in hard times. Why? Your faith will grow when it faces resistance. Like a muscle that needs exercised and strengthened, your faith is built by trials. As you suffer more and more, you'll grow in endurance. And all that endurance will help complete you. It might not make sense and it definitely won't feel comfortable, but enduring trials and suffering will make you stronger in the long run.

---

*Father, I don't like the thought of needing to grow in
endurance. And I don't want to welcome suffering
in my life. Even though I don't enjoy trials, it's pretty
amazing that You use them to shape me into
a better, stronger woman. Please help me lean
into the process and trust You completely.*

HELP THAT'S ALWAYS PRESENT

God is our refuge and strength,
an ever-present help in trouble.

PSALM 46:1 NIV

When you contemplate headlines in the news, you can learn plenty of lessons. For one, you shouldn't place your hope in things of this world. Another lesson is that anything can happen, so you need to remember that your plans are only possibilities and not certainties. Yet another lesson is that God alone should be your refuge and strength—not people or leaders or institutions.

Things of this world can create a diversion, but they'll never be a true refuge like the Lord. Once you embrace what a strong protection and help the Lord alone is, you can face your troubles. In fact, you can face *anything* with His help and strength that's always present. Your own strength will fail you, but God's strength never will.

Father God, You are my refuge in this uncertain
world. You are my strength when everything around
me seems to crumble. You are always there to
help me, even in times of trouble. Thank You!

ONE MIND AND ONE VOICE

May the God who gives endurance and encouragement
give you the same attitude of mind toward each other that
Christ Jesus had, so that with one mind and one voice you
may glorify the God and Father of our Lord Jesus Christ.

ROMANS 15:5–6 NIV

Unity doesn't happen automatically. And when you face differences of opinion with others, it can seem pretty difficult and even impossible to come together in unity. But unity is exactly what the Lord wants for His believers.

The fantastic news is you're not left on your own to try to stay unified. Just as the Lord can turn your suffering into endurance, He can give you the same attitude of mind toward other believers. And as you unite with one similar mind and one similar voice, you'll glorify Him. He can unite your heart with the hearts of other believers in amazing ways.

Lord God, thank You for the good, unexplainable ways
You unite Your followers. Please help me be open to
the way You can and will move. I don't want to get in
the way of what You want to do in me and through
me. I want You to create unity in my whole life.

IT MAKES ME SICK

"Look, O Lord, for I am in distress;
my stomach churns; my heart is wrung
within me, because I have been very rebellious."

LAMENTATIONS 1:20 ESV

When something awful happens, feeling sick to your stomach is a natural reaction. You might not be sure exactly how bad news makes you feel nauseated, but it does. Your stomach churns and feels like it's tied in knots. Your heart feels like it's breaking and wrung out. Your mouth might feel really dry, or your hands get clammy or shaky.

When you rebel and willfully choose to sin, the Holy Spirit will convict you in such a way that you'll feel distressed. You'll feel sick to your stomach. Your heart will hurt. While you can't keep bad things from happening to you, you can choose not to sin. As you obey the Lord and follow His leading, you won't experience so many physical effects tied to sin and guilt and shame.

Father, at times obedience feels difficult, but following
Your righteous way protects me from so much. When I
rebel, I feel bad. My choices bring real, physical effects.
Help me discern Your truth and follow Your way!

HOLINESS

As obedient children, do not conform to the evil
desires you had when you lived in ignorance. But just
as he who called you is holy, so be holy in all you
do; for it is written: "Be holy, because I am holy."

1 PETER 1:14–16 NIV

Holiness seems so unattainable. Maybe once you praise the Lord for His holiness, it's hard to imagine yourself coming anywhere close to His sacredness. Holy living seems out of reach when you're surrounded by everyday life.

Yet the apostle Peter connected holiness to obedience. As an obedient daughter of your heavenly Father, don't be like the world. You don't have to live in ignorance anymore. You can break free from evil desires you had before coming to Christ. Because your heavenly Father is holy and because He has called you, you can be holy in all you do. Pursue a life of holiness because He is holy. In doing so, you'll free yourself from so many of the world's constraints and enjoy the liberty of living in Christ.

Father, I want to be holy because You are holy.
Even if it seems impossible in this sinful world,
I know all things are possible through You.

MAKE THE MOST OF IT!

Be wise in the way you act toward outsiders;
make the most of every opportunity.

COLOSSIANS 4:5 NIV

Feeling consumed by the busyness of life? When you're bombarded by requests and expectations from other people, sometimes it's necessary to create boundaries. It's also tempting to zone out. Yet, in any situation, believers are called to pay attention and make the most of every opportunity.

Overwhelm or distractions or a lack of energy shouldn't stop your entire world. Pay attention to your surroundings and pray for discernment. When God opens your eyes to unique opportunities with outsiders, don't be afraid to step out in faith and share Christ's love in kindness. With kindness and respect, speak the truth in love. Even in the middle of an overwhelming day, decide to let your light shine for Christ. Be a beacon of hope in this dark world.

Lord Jesus, help me look for the opportunities You give
me to love others well. As I do, please give me Your words
and Your kindness to make a difference in this world.

REFRESHMENT

A generous person will prosper;
whoever refreshes others will be refreshed.
PROVERBS 11:25 NIV

Being willing to give is a beautiful thing. You might have a little to give or you might be able to give a lot, but the amount isn't important. What really does matter? Your kindness, thoughtfulness, and generosity. Not only will you bless others through your willingness to give, but you'll also be blessed in the process.

If you stop to think about it, a generous life involves giving out of an abundance. You're not stingy, and you don't selfishly cling to things. Rather, you're willing to give something away. You might give your time. You could give material gifts like food or belongings or money. Possibilities for generous living and giving are endless— all you need to do is consider how you could step into someone else's world and bless them. When you do, you'll be a welcome refreshment to someone else. You might be surprised with the way your giving refreshes you too.

Father, You're so generous to pour out grace
upon grace to me. Please help me follow Your
example to be kind and generous to others.

THE ADDICTION OF PRIDE

"Whoever exalts himself will be humbled,
and whoever humbles himself will be exalted."
MATTHEW 23:12 ESV

In this social media–saturated world, where selfies and status updates consume thoughts and time, it might be the easiest moment in history to exalt yourself. Whether you realize it or not, if you scrutinize your photos to see if they're worth sharing with others, you're exalting yourself. Along with some self-exaltation, your social media swipes and likes fuel a dopamine fix; and all that dopamine creates an addiction.

Aside from the serious issues that come with addiction, it's time to consider where you're seeking your validation and attention. It's also time to consider how self-importance has forced its way into your thoughts.

The Bible is crystal clear when it comes to this issue: whoever exalts herself will be humbled. The Lord opposes the proud but gives grace to the humble. Not only is it time to stop exalting yourself, but it's also time to exalt the King of kings and Lord of lords. He's the One worthy of your attention.

Father, please forgive me for focusing on myself. Please help
me break my sinful habits! Please help me stop following
the ways of the world. I want to exalt You and You alone.

WORTHY OF IMITATION

Therefore be imitators of God, as beloved children.
And walk in love, as Christ loved us and gave himself
up for us, a fragrant offering and sacrifice to God.
EPHESIANS 5:1–2 ESV

When you're at a loss for ideas—whether it's for decorating your home or shopping for a new outfit or brainstorming gift possibilities or planning a special meal—it's fun to look for inspiration. In fact, it's easy to get sucked into Pinterest, HGTV, and plenty of blogs for hours.

Imitating and finding inspiration from others is a great way to expand your own horizons. But when it comes to living life, there's no one better to imitate than God Himself. As His beloved daughter, it's really good to imitate your Father.

His Son, Jesus, walked on this earth and gave us a perfect example to follow. What was one of His biggest wishes? That His followers would imitate His love. He asked those who choose to follow Him to walk in love and unity. As you love others, you'll imitate the only One worth imitating.

Father God, I'm so thankful You're worth imitating.
Thank You for sending Jesus into this world as a real-life
example of how I should live and love. Please help
me imitate Him and His amazing sacrificial love.

BREAKING THE CYCLE

I lift up my eyes to the hills. From where does my help come? My help comes from the LORD, who made heaven and earth.

PSALM 121:1–2 ESV

How many times do you find yourself falling into the same cycle of anxiety, overwhelm, then procrastination? This feeling of getting stuck and staying stuck is frustrating, and it can happen in just about every area of life.

The fantastic news is you don't have to stay stuck. There's a way to get past the anxiety and overwhelm and procrastination, but it's not found in five simple steps or a self-help plan. Freedom comes from the Lord. He's the One who will pull you out. He's the One who will set you in a sturdy spot and help you move forward. Lift your eyes to Him and ask for help. He's the One who will help you break the cycle!

Father, my help comes from You. You made heaven and earth, and You made me. Please help me break out of this cycle of frustration, anxiety, overwhelm, and defeat!

THE CURE FOR OVERWHELM

*Rejoice always, pray without ceasing, in everything give
thanks; for this is the will of God for you in Christ Jesus.*

1 THESSALONIANS 5:16–18 NASB

Overwhelm doesn't always have one single cause. Sometimes all kinds of things add together until you're faced with too much all at once. You're dealing with sibling squabbles and driving teens to after-school jobs and remembering to pick up dog food and returning clothes to the store and figuring out what's for dinner—all while getting texts that steal your attention and focus. The never-ending demands and constant diversion of attention lead to overwhelm. It's not like you face just a single day of overwhelm; this happens day after day after day.

Even when overwhelm leaves your mind spinning, the Bible offers a very different response than what you may be tempted to do. Rejoice always, even in the middle of the demands of life. Pray without ceasing. And in everything—even when your day's been filled with a clogged toilet and furnace repairs and traffic jams—give thanks. All this rejoicing and prayer and thankfulness is God's will for you. It's what will help you survive and thrive through overwhelm.

---

*Father, I praise You that Your will for me in Christ Jesus is
joy and prayer and thanksgiving. What a sweet relief!*

GETTING OUT OF THE MUCK

*I waited patiently for the LORD; he turned to me
and heard my cry. He lifted me out of the slimy
pit, out of the mud and mire; he set my feet on
a rock and gave me a firm place to stand.*

PSALM 40:1–2 NIV

When you're surrounded by overwhelming circumstances, it's easy to feel like you're sinking deep into quicksand. No matter what you try, there's no way out. What can you do to break free? How can you get back to some sense of normalcy?

The Psalms cover a wide range of emotions like doubt, disappointment, despair, and overwhelm. So what did the psalmist do when he felt like he was stuck in the muck and mire? He cried out to the Lord; then he patiently waited. How the Lord responded to the psalmist's cries for help should give hope to everyone. He turned and heard the cries. He lifted the psalmist out of the slimy pit. He set his feet on a strong and sturdy rock, giving a safe and sure place to stand.

Just as the Lord acted in the psalmist's life, He can act in your life too. Cry out to Him and patiently wait. Watch the way He'll lift you out of the slimy pit, set your feet on a rock, and give you a firm place to stand.

*Father, please help me! Please get me out of this sticky,
miry mess and set me in a safe, steady place.*

RUN YOUR RACE

*Therefore, since we are surrounded by such a great cloud
of witnesses, let us throw off everything that hinders
and the sin that so easily entangles. And let us run
with perseverance the race marked out for us, fixing
our eyes on Jesus, the pioneer and perfecter of faith.*

HEBREWS 12:1–2 NIV

So often, overwhelm feels like you're caught in a trap. Like getting caught in a net, as much as you try to break free, you find yourself more and more tangled. Overwhelm feels that way, and sin does too. And if you're caught in a sin cycle, as much as you try to break free, you might get more and more tangled.

While you could try to break free on your own and wait until every tangle is gone, you also could try the Bible's advice. Look to Jesus and set your eyes on Him. He created your faith, and He's perfecting it even now through a course set just for you to run. When you look at how someone else is running, it's easy to veer off course. Put the comparison game away! Instead, choose to persevere and run the race that Christ has marked out just for you.

---

*Lord Jesus, thank You for setting a race just for me.
I want to look to You as I run. Please help me keep
my eyes on You for direction and inspiration.*

GUARD YOUR HEART

Above all else, guard your heart,
for everything you do flows from it.
PROVERBS 4:23 NIV

Have you ever considered that the overwhelming aspects of your life may not even need to be there in the first place? It's so easy to try to take on anything that comes your way without considering if you *should* take it on. By trying to fix everything or be all things for all people, you end up taking on so much more than is necessary.

So what's the solution? How do you stop involving yourself in everything? Start by guarding your heart. As you do, you'll be able to discern what really needs your attention and involvement. Then, when you know what you shouldn't take on, be bold and create a boundary. Guard your heart and stick to what's necessary for you.

Father, please give me wisdom and discernment
to know what I need to concentrate on and what
I should leave out. Please help me guard my heart
as a way to prevent feeling so overwhelmed.

NO EXCUSE

Therefore, rid yourselves of all malice and all deceit, hypocrisy, envy, and slander of every kind. Like newborn babies, crave pure spiritual milk, so that by it you may grow up in your salvation, now that you have tasted that the Lord is good.

1 Peter 2:1–3 NIV

Feeling overwhelmed can lead to so many reactions you'd rather not experience. You might say something you truly didn't mean to say. You might erupt in anger. You might snap at the kindest, most well-meaning people.

The thing is, feeling overwhelmed isn't an excuse to vent and misbehave. It's not a free pass for a nasty attitude. In his letter to fellow believers, Peter revealed that Christ followers need to crave spiritual milk and grow up in their salvation. When you grow up in your salvation, it means you need to get rid of certain things that were part of your former way of living. You need to get rid of malice and deceit. You need to get rid of hypocrisy, envy, and any kind of slander.

Consider what you say and do, whether you're feeling overwhelmed or not.

Father, I want to grow up in my salvation! I want to get rid of all the awful aspects of who I was before I trusted in Christ. Please help me not use overwhelm as an excuse to make bad choices.

WORKING HARD?

*We know that a person is not justified by works of
the law but through faith in Jesus Christ, so we also
have believed in Christ Jesus, in order to be justified by
faith in Christ and not by works of the law, because
by works of the law no one will be justified.*
GALATIANS 2:16 ESV

If you're generally a hard worker, it's easy to let that worker's attitude seep into every aspect of your life. Instead of just limiting your diligence to work at your job or around your home, you might think you need to diligently work for a better standing with Christ.

Faith in Jesus means that you don't have to work for your salvation. Faith in Him and His sacrificial act of saving you is all you need. You're not justified or saved by the things you do. You're not made right with Christ by working harder or doing more. Faith and belief in Christ alone is how you're saved. You can breathe a deep sigh of relief and stop trying to work so hard to gain your Savior's favor.

*Christ Jesus, thank You for Your amazing gift of
grace! Thank You that You alone are the One who
saves me. It doesn't matter what I do or don't
do. You are the only One who can save me.*

THE DIFFERENCE A
RIGHT CHOICE MAKES

*I was young and now I am old, yet I have never
seen the righteous forsaken or their children
begging bread. They are always generous and
lend freely; their children will be a blessing.*

PSALM 37:25–26 NIV

No matter how overwhelmed you might feel, you always
need to choose how you'll live. Do you make righteous
decisions that are virtuous and equitable? Or, if you're
feeling stressed, do you cut corners and let sin creep into
your choices?

Regardless of your stress level, keep choosing righteousness. Proverbs 21:21 (NIV) teaches, "Whoever pursues
righteousness and love finds life, prosperity and honor."
And in Psalm 37, the psalmist shared the truth about the
way God treats the righteous. God provides and cares for
them and their families. The righteous are never forsaken.
In fact, they always have enough to generously share with
others. Keep making righteous choices, and watch the way
the Lord will lovingly provide for you and your family.

---

*Father, it's such a relief to know You love and care
for those who are righteous in Your sight. I pray
I'll live a life of virtue, even if it seems difficult,
and I pray I'll generously give to others.*

LOSING IT

Then Jesus said to his disciples, "Whoever wants to be my disciple must deny themselves and take up their cross and follow me. For whoever wants to save their life will lose it, but whoever loses their life for me will find it."

MATTHEW 16:24–25 NIV

How many people go through life determined to make certain things happen? It might be as innocent as crossing off items on a bucket list or as intense as setting outrageous goals and hustling until you drop from exhaustion.

As you live your life, setting goals and recognizing your hopes isn't bad. In fact, when made prayerfully, goals can help you set a good direction. But if you find yourself obsessing over what you want to accomplish, you may not be letting the Lord step in to guide and direct you in the way He wants you to go.

Jesus has asked for self-denial from those of us who want to follow Him. So follow Him, and lose the life you *think* you should lead. As you do, you'll truly find your life.

Lord Jesus, I do want to be Your disciple! Even if it's difficult, I want to deny myself. I want to follow You and lose my life for Your sake.

HIS GREAT LOVE

But because of his great love for us, God, who is rich in mercy, made us alive with Christ even when we were dead in transgressions—it is by grace you have been saved.

EPHESIANS 2:4–5 NIV

Realizing all the weaknesses that come along with humanity can be so frustrating. Perfection seems like it should be attainable if you just try enough or work hard enough. But everyone has flaws and failures. No one's an unstoppable superhero with unlimited strength and abilities.

Every single person sins and falls short of the glory of God. But God, in His great mercy, stepped in with a solution. He chose to send His Son, Jesus, to save the world. Even when our sins kept us apart from God and His holy perfection, Jesus came to save us. It's this undeserved gift of love that saves us from the punishment of our sins. We're made alive in Him and through Him, all because of His great love.

Father, thank You for the great love You have for me! Thank You for being so merciful. Thank You for sending Jesus as the rescue for sinful people like me. I'm grateful for His sacrifice!

GIVE ME SOME SHELTER

But let all who take refuge in you be glad; let them ever sing for joy. Spread your protection over them, that those who love your name may rejoice in you. Surely, LORD, you bless the righteous; you surround them with your favor as with a shield.

PSALM 5:11–12 NIV

It's hard to live in this world. While it can be a beautiful place filled with blessing, so much is broken and corrupt after the fall in the Garden of Eden. What was made to be good is tainted by sin.

When life feels hard and you're overwhelmed by relentless storms and trials, take shelter in the Lord. Let Him be the refuge you run to, your safe haven when life comes crashing down. As you run to Him, rejoice that you can. Be glad that you know and worship the mighty God. Hide yourself in the shelter of His wings, and sing for joy. Enjoy His favor that protects you from the dangers of this life. Soak in His blessings, and know that He is good. Believe that His loving-kindness is better than life and that it endures forever.

Lord God, I come to You for shelter from the storms of this world. When life feels overwhelming, I trust You. Thank You for Your favor and Your protection. I love You and rejoice in You.

WATCH THE CHANGES

For God has not given us a spirit of timidity,
but of power and love and discipline.
2 TIMOTHY 1:7 NASB

When you come to the Lord and begin walking with Him in your everyday life, things don't stay the same. You're not the same person you'd be without Him. For one thing, He fills you with His Holy Spirit—that's God living in you. The almighty God, maker of heaven and earth, empowers you.

You can imagine that the all-powerful God doesn't lead you to a life of fear or timidity. No, He fills you with His bold power. You're brimming with His love and can't help but share with others. He also gives you the great gift of discipline, so you're not living an out-of-control, haphazard sort of life.

As He lives in you, lean into the power, love, and discipline He supplies. Watch how He changes you and works in you.

Father, it's amazing to know You'll give me boldness I don't have on my own. You'll help me love others when I feel like I can't. And You'll bring discipline into my life instead of a mess. Thank You for Your Holy Spirit and the way He lives and works and moves in me.

GUILTY!

My guilt has overwhelmed me
like a burden too heavy to bear.
PSALM 38:4 NIV

Guilt brings a burden that weighs you down like a heavy load. Unable to bear the weight on your own, you feel trapped. Overwhelmed by regret, you're enslaved in a nasty prison of guilt.

Yet there is hope. There's a freedom from the burden of guilt, and it comes from Christ alone. He has paid the penalty for your sin. And when you believe in Him and ask Him to take the punishment of your sin away, He does.

He's already done the brutal job for you. Offering His very life as a sacrifice, He paid the price for all you've done wrong. Once you admit you need Him and you gladly accept what He's offered, forgiveness and freedom are yours. Break the chains of your guilt. Find freedom from the burden of your sins, and accept Christ's free gift.

Lord Jesus, thank You! Thank You for taking what
was simply too heavy for me to bear. Thank
You for freeing me from the penalty of my sins.
Thank You for setting me free from my guilt.

COME AWAY

*And He said to them, "Come away by yourselves to
a secluded place and rest a little while." (For there
were many people coming and going, and they did
not even have time to eat.) And they went away
in the boat to a secluded place by themselves.*

MARK 6:31–32 NASB

If anyone ever had a reason to be overwhelmed, it would
have been Jesus. Surrounded by demanding crowds all the
time, He regularly faced opposition from religious leaders,
performed miracles, and shepherded His disciples.

What was Jesus' secret to dealing with potential overwhelm? Retreating from everyone and spending some
time in solitude. He needed to wake up very early to do
it, but this was His vital secret. He passed this coping
strategy along to His disciples too, when He encouraged
them to come away by themselves to a secluded place so
they could rest.

Just like Jesus taught, make seclusion and rest a priority. Intentionally add rest into your life. Get away by
yourself to meet with your heavenly Father. You'll be able
to deal with the demands of life much easier when you're
refreshed and rested.

---

*Lord Jesus, I'm so grateful for the example You
set for everyone. Like You, I want to make rest
a priority. Please remind me to get away by
myself to a secluded place so I can rest awhile.*

HOPE IN HIM

"The LORD is my portion," says my soul,
"therefore I will hope in him."
LAMENTATIONS 3:24 ESV

When the book of Lamentations explains that we can hope in the Lord because He's our portion, it sounds nice and biblical. But what in the world does it mean? We know what it is to hope in the Lord. But how is He our portion?

The Lord is your share. He's your possession. He's your inheritance. He's your reward. He's your lot in life. He's all you have. He's all you need, and you can depend on Him. He's your portion.

Because He's your everything, you can hope in Him. You don't have to hope in yourself or anyone or anything else in this world. When life overwhelms and seems to suck the life and joy out of you, remember who He is. Hope in Him!

Father God, You are my everything! I'm so
thankful You're my reward. Please help
me live for You. You are all I need.

JUST PASSING THROUGH

*Dear friends, I urge you, as foreigners and exiles,
to abstain from sinful desires, which
wage war against your soul.*

1 PETER 2:11 NIV

Living in this world, but not settling in like you're part of this world, can seem a little tricky. Depending on the company you keep or where you live, you may feel sucked into living like everyone else around you. But if that way of living focuses on worldly pursuits instead of things that honor and glorify the Lord, then you're being led astray.

In his letter, Peter urged Christ followers to turn away from sinful desires. And why? Those desires wage war against your soul.

As a believer of the one true God, you can live this life knowing you're not meant to stay here. You're a foreigner and an exile in this world. You're waiting until the day you can head to your forever home. Like a traveler in a foreign country, you may feel like unpacking your suitcase, but know that you're not staying here forever. There's no need to settle in.

---

*Father, why is it so hard to remember I'm just
passing through this world? Please help me not
get comfortable and settle into a life of sin. I
want to live a life that's set apart for You.*

EVERY NEED

And my God will supply every need of yours
according to his riches in glory in Christ Jesus.
PHILIPPIANS 4:19 ESV

Wants and needs can be so different. Depending on your season of life, you may want a lot of things. Until you reach a point of contentment, it can be difficult to discern between what you want and what you truly need.

And sometimes, you know exactly what you need, but the needs may feel like they're huge asks. Never in a million years could you provide some of your needs on your own. In those moments, when you feel overwhelmed and wonder how in the world you'll make it on your own, remember that God can take care of you and supply all your needs. He won't let you eke by but will generously and graciously supply all your needs according to His riches in glory. Those glorious riches are far better than anything you can provide for yourself.

When you're feeling desperate and know what you need, tell Him about it. Ask for Him to provide, and then rest in trust.

Lord God, You are good to me. You own the cattle on a thousand hills, and You're more than capable of providing for me. Please meet my needs. They seem overwhelming to me, but I know I can trust You to completely provide for me.

LET ME PONDER THIS

The heart of the righteous ponders how to answer,
but the mouth of the wicked pours out evil things.
PROVERBS 15:28 NASB

When you're stressed to the point of overwhelm, it is so easy to snap at other people. It doesn't matter who seeks your attention or what they're talking about—overwhelm has a way of creating a very short fuse.

The book of Proverbs specifies there's a righteous and unrighteous way to deal with speech, and not surprisingly, the righteous way doesn't involve a short fuse. Instead of flying off the handle or being quick to anger, a righteous person ponders her answer first. She takes her time to consider different responses. The unrighteous, wicked person just pours out trash talk. Evil things—comments and statements that cut to the core and hurt others—come flying out of the mouth of the wicked.

As you pursue a life that's right in the Lord's eyes, ponder your answers before opening your mouth. Listeners will be much better off because of your discretion.

Father, I want to be righteous in Your sight. Please
help me hold my tongue and think before I speak.

WHAT'S INSIDE?

*"A good man brings good things out of the good
stored up in him, and an evil man brings evil
things out of the evil stored up in him."*

MATTHEW 12:35 NIV

Trying to balance multiple roles in life can feel brutal. It's exhausting to focus on working, caring for your family, caring for your home, running errands, volunteering, and trying to fit in some time for yourself. Any one task requires a lot of details, but when you need to juggle plenty of things? The demands escalate in a hurry.

All that busyness will quickly reveal what's in your heart. If you're a good woman and are walking closely with the Lord, good things will come out of the good stored up in you. But if you have no relationship with Him? Expect bad things to bubble out.

You'd be surprised to open a pristine-looking box and find a bunch of moldy garbage inside. You'd also be shocked to find a disgusting, dilapidated box filled with well-kept, priceless treasures. Just like those boxes, a good, righteous person won't be filled with a bunch of rotting junk. And an evil person won't be filled with goodness. When you're busy balancing life, your true character will be revealed. Will you discover good treasures? Or awful junk?

*Father, I want to be a good, righteous follower
of Christ! I want good things to come out
of the good that's stored up in me.*

WORTHY

*As a prisoner for the Lord, then, I urge you to live
a life worthy of the calling you have received. Be
completely humble and gentle; be patient, bearing
with one another in love. Make every effort to keep
the unity of the Spirit through the bond of peace.*

EPHESIANS 4:1–3 NIV

Do you know you've received a calling? There, in the middle
of your everyday life, the Lord has called you to Himself.
Through Jesus, He offers forgiveness and salvation. Along
with His amazing gift of salvation, He's planned good
works for you to do too.

Since you've been called by Him, how should you live?
The apostle Paul was quick to explain to Ephesian believers
what it looks like to live a life worthy of the calling you've
received. You need to be completely humble. (Goodbye,
pride!) You need to be gentle and not harsh. You need to
be patient. In love, you need to bear with other people.
And through peace, you need to make every effort to keep
the unity of the Spirit.

That life of love, peace, patience, gentleness, and humility sounds a lot like a life that overflows with the fruit
of the Spirit. As you let the Holy Spirit work through you,
His fruit will be evident in your life.

*Lord, thank You for Your Holy Spirit! I pray He will lead
me to live a life worthy of the calling You've given me.*

ONE STEP AT A TIME

*Direct my footsteps according to your
word; let no sin rule over me.*
PSALM 119:133 NIV

Do you get frustrated when you need to make a decision but have no idea what's the best choice? When you're feeling confused, having some idea of the final destination would be nice. If you only knew how things would work out, you could make better decisions now.

Yet life's not like that. You're not meant to know what's coming in the future. Life is like a journey down a road, so consider the beautiful truth that God's Word is a lamp to your feet and a light to your path. Like a flashlight, a lamp lights your way so you can take the next step without tripping or falling. It's not a searchlight or a spotlight. You don't need to know where you'll be making a turn five miles down the road.

Keep taking one step at a time with the Lord, and try to rest in the fact that you don't need all the answers ahead of time. Be grateful for the way He leads and guides, and pray that He will continue to direct your footsteps.

*Father God, thank You for Your Word and the way
it gives me direction. Please continue to guide
me in the way I should go today. I want to trust
You as I walk step by step through life.*

ASK AND IT WILL BE GIVEN

If any of you lacks wisdom, you should ask
God, who gives generously to all without
finding fault, and it will be given to you.

JAMES 1:5 NIV

All sorts of responsibilities and to-dos have a way of piling up. Knowing you need to place God first in your life, juggle incessant everyday chores and schedules, and work hard just to keep up with the never-ending bills *seems* like a lot because it *is* a lot. All those needs and responsibilities are necessary parts of life. But how do you muster enough time or energy to do it all day after day after day?

James offered a solution: ask God for wisdom! When you don't know how to juggle it all, ask the Lord. When you're not sure what is necessary, ask God. Ask Him for wisdom in your daily responsibilities and tasks, and He will generously give it. Ask and it will be given to you.

Father, I need Your help! Please give me wisdom to
discern what I need to do. I want to do what's right
in Your eyes, but I have no idea what that might be.

HOW GREAT IS YOUR GOD

The salvation of the righteous comes from the LORD; he is their stronghold in time of trouble. The LORD helps them and delivers them; he delivers them from the wicked and saves them, because they take refuge in him.

PSALM 37:39–40 NIV

As a woman, you know your weaknesses and strengths. You know that even your strongest strengths will give way at some point.

But take a moment to consider the Lord. He has no weaknesses—as in *absolutely none*. Because He is a God of complete strength, He can be your stronghold in times of trouble. When other people fail you, He never will. When disappointments crush you, He'll never disappoint. He saves you in an irreversible way. He'll help you. He'll deliver you. When you trust in Him and look to Him for safety and refuge, He will follow through every single time.

No one and nothing is as dependable as the Lord. No one and nothing can save you for eternity like He can.

My Lord and my God, I worship You. You truly are magnificent, and it's a gift to be known by You. Thank You for Your saving grace. Thank You for being my stronghold in the absolute worst times of my life. Thank You for Your incredible deliverance.

PARENTING UNCERTAINTIES

When Joseph and Mary saw Him, they were bewildered;
and His mother said to Him, "Son, why have You treated
us this way? Behold, Your father and I have been anxiously
looking for You!" And He said to them, "Why is it that you
were looking for Me? Did you not know that I had to be
in My Father's house?" And yet they on their part did not
understand the statement which He had made to them.

LUKE 2:48–50 NASB

Before you become a mom, parenting looks like it should be easy. If your child behaves a certain way, there should be a simple correction. But motherhood is anything but easy. Because of temperaments and unique situations, a lot of thought is needed for most issues.

Mary, the mother of Jesus, knew this firsthand. Even when Jesus was doing what He needed to do, it caught both Mary and Joseph by surprise. Unaware of where their preteen son was, Mary and Joseph anxiously searched until they found Him. When they discovered Him at the temple, they were bewildered. And when He told them why He was there, they couldn't understand Jesus' reasoning.

At times, parenting is bewildering. You won't always understand what your children think or do. They won't understand you. You'll experience moments of anxiety. Just know you're not alone. This isn't unique to your family—even Jesus' parents experienced this.

Lord, I'm not sure why You've created the dynamics of
parenting the way You have, but I'm thankful I'm not
alone. Please give me wisdom as I raise my children!

HARD WORK

Those who work their land will have abundant food,
but those who chase fantasies have no sense.
PROVERBS 12:11 NIV

Hard work is a really good thing. Sometimes it's difficult to feel motivated to work hard. Other times, you simply might be exhausted. But continuing to work, whether you feel like it or not, is wise.

Proverbs explains one of the benefits to diligent work: you'll have abundant food! If you work and keep working, you'll be able to provide for yourself, including necessities like food. But if you refuse to work, you can forget about an abundance of food.

If you find yourself chasing fantasies, you'll want to change your habits. A diligent, hardworking outlook will get you much further in life than daydreaming and doing a bunch of nothing. Even if hard work is tiring, it's a really good thing with great rewards.

Father, please help me experience the benefits
of working hard. When I feel tired, please give me
energy and strength to keep working for Your glory.

RIGHT FROM WRONG

*For what credit is there if, when you sin and are
harshly treated, you endure it with patience? But
if when you do what is right and suffer for it you
patiently endure it, this finds favor with God.*

1 PETER 2:20 NASB

At some point in your life, you'll suffer. Everyone does.
To navigate through your suffering, you'll need to endure.
Suffering and endurance are necessary parts of life, so the
bigger issue is what your attitude will be in the middle
of suffering. And why will you suffer? Will you suffer for
something wrong you did? Or will you suffer for doing
right?

While everyone lives with regrets, it's important to
remember that God wants you to do good. He's pleased
when you make right choices and live a righteous kind of
life. While He's willing to forgive you when you sin and
fall short of perfection, He's pleased when you choose to
do what's virtuous. Insomuch that you can control what
you do, choose to do what's right. Even if you end up
suffering for that choice and need to patiently endure,
you'll find favor with the Lord.

*Father, please open my eyes so I can clearly see
what's right and what's wrong. Help me boldly
and bravely choose to do the right thing.*

WALK WORTHY

Walk in a manner worthy of the Lord, fully pleasing to him: bearing fruit in every good work and increasing in the knowledge of God; being strengthened with all power, according to his glorious might.

COLOSSIANS 1:10–11 ESV

The thought of living in a manner worthy of the Lord is intimidating. You're only human! You know your weaknesses better than anyone else. You know your temptations and your tendencies. How can you walk in a manner that's fully pleasing to Him?

The apostle Paul gave a list of God-honoring practices to focus on, but they don't come naturally. You'll need to stay focused and make it a point to live in this worthy way. For starters, do good. With every good work you do, you'll end up bearing fruit. Increase your knowledge of God. Read and study the Bible. Pray. Know your Maker. Find your strength in Him and not yourself. As you do, you'll be strengthened with His power and glorious might so you can endure with patience and joy.

Father, I want to walk in a manner that's worthy of You! I want to please You! Please help me bear Your fruit and increase in my knowledge of You. I want to be strengthened with Your power.

REALLY GOOD THINGS

*Certainly goodness and faithfulness will follow
me all the days of my life, and my dwelling
will be in the house of the LORD forever.*

PSALM 23:6 NASB

When the Lord is your shepherd, really good things happen. You won't be in want. He'll restore your soul. He'll guide you in righteous ways. You don't have to fear, because He is with you and will comfort you. He'll protect you and abundantly provide for you. Even when circumstances don't seem like they could be favorable, goodness and faithfulness will follow you every single day. And when your life on earth is over, you'll dwell and fellowship with the Lord forever.

All of those amazing, really good things are yours, but you have to choose to follow the Good Shepherd instead of your own ways. Instead of being stubborn or insisting on your own independence, let Him gently lead you. You'll never regret following His path.

---

*Lord, You are the Good Shepherd. Thank You for seeking
me out. I don't have to stray from You. You willingly
lead me so I experience many wonderful things.*

PROCESSING BAD NEWS

Now when Jesus heard about John, He withdrew
from there in a boat to a secluded place by
Himself; and when the people heard about this,
they followed Him on foot from the cities.

MATTHEW 14:13 NASB

Hopefully, it's not too often that you get life-changing, devastating news. Even if you expect to hear bad news, it's never easy to process or accept.

Jesus demonstrated a helpful way to deal with bad news after He heard that His cousin John the Baptist had been beheaded: He withdrew. He left everyone behind and retreated to a secluded place.

When you need to pray through and process news that brings you to your knees in pain and shock and grief, get away from people and responsibilities. Withdraw by yourself and retreat with the Lord. Start to deal with your thoughts and feelings before going back to the normal pace of life.

Lord Jesus, during Your life on earth, You modeled such
effective ways to deal with all that humans face. Thank You
for showing me how to deal with grief and awful news.

OLD AND NEW

*You were taught, with regard to your former way of
life, to put off your old self, which is being corrupted
by its deceitful desires; to be made new in the attitude
of your minds; and to put on the new self, created to
be like God in true righteousness and holiness.*

 EPHESIANS 4:22–24 NIV

Have you ever bought much-needed new clothing like
socks or underwear because your old clothing was so old
and worn it was holey? When you brought your new items
home, did you discard the old items right away, or did you
keep wearing them?

Just like worn-out clothing deserves to be pitched,
your life and habits before you accepted Christ need a
thorough decluttering. If you've been saved by the grace
of God, live like it! Get rid of anything that resembles
your former way of living. Put off your old self and get a
fresh, new start. Have a fresh, clean, brand-new attitude.
Make right choices that are holy in the sight of the Lord.
As you do, you'll live like the person you truly are, and not
a shadow of who you used to be.

*God Almighty, thank You for offering me a new
life when I come to Christ. Please help my body
and mind reflect my new life in You. I want to
put off my old self and put on my new self!*

GRIEVING AND MOURNING

Be merciful to me, LORD, for I am in distress; my eyes
grow weak with sorrow, my soul and body with grief.

PSALM 31:9 NIV

Grieving and mourning is an overwhelming process that
feels like it may never end. When you're so completely
overcome by sorrow, nothing feels like it will improve.
Nothing could be normal again.

As you grieve, cry out to the Lord. Plead to Him for
mercy. Admit you're in distress and honestly pour out all
your thoughts to Him. Let your tears flow. As you cry
and cry until your eyes are weak with sorrow, ask Him for
comfort. Ask Him for peace. Even when your soul feels
overcome by grief, share everything with the Lord. Vent
your anger. Wail with sorrow. Weep and moan with grief.
As you get all your feelings out, look to Him for comfort
and hope. Out of His great love and compassion, He'll
respond in mercy.

Father, I am speechless. My sorrow consumes me.
I beg for mercy, Lord. Please show mercy to me.

MAKING TIME

*Do your best to present yourself to God as one
approved, a worker who has no need to be
ashamed, rightly handling the word of truth.*

2 TIMOTHY 2:15 ESV

Tasks and responsibilities have a way of crowding out what you need the most. Urgent requests can pop up every day. But unless you're truly facing an emergency, don't drop everything to tend to what *seems* to be urgent. A smarter, more effective plan is to make sure you do a couple of vital things each day. Focus on completing these major priorities, and watch everything else fall into place.

One of these priorities may be to take time alone with the Lord. As you sit at His feet, through prayer and reading His Word, your relationship with Him will continue to grow deeper and richer. As you prioritize time with your Father each day, you'll begin to rightly handle the Word of truth. You'll also have a better idea of how to best present yourself to God as one approved. All this starts when you make time for Him.

---

*Father, please help me prioritize my time with You so I get
to know You more deeply and worship You more regularly.
I don't want the urgent to crowd out what's truly important!*

A BROKEN HEART

The LORD is close to the brokenhearted
and saves those who are crushed in spirit.

PSALM 34:18 NIV

It's funny how having a broken heart actually feels like
your heart has broken. It really, really hurts deep inside.
And when your spirit has been crushed, it feels like actual
crushing pain. Your mental and physical health are connected in a powerful way.

A painful burden seems like something you can only
bear alone. Yet you're not truly alone. The Lord is close to
the brokenhearted. Knowing everything you've experienced
and felt, He wants to help. He saves those who are crushed
in spirit. Call out to Him. He knows that your grief is
overwhelming you. He's there to comfort your spirit. Wait
for the peace that comes from the Lord.

Lord of sorrows, please help my broken heart! I feel so
overwhelmed by grief, like I can barely breathe. I don't
know how to go on. Please help me. I want to know You're
there. I long for Your comfort and peace. I need You to step
in and save my crushed spirit. Please have mercy on me!

LIFE

Whoever believes in the Son has eternal life,
but whoever rejects the Son will not see life,
for God's wrath remains on them.

JOHN 3:36 NIV

Rooted deep inside humans is the need to ponder the meaning of life. Throughout history, some people have created their own religions to explain what they think life must be about—and what might happen after death.

Christianity's the only religion where followers worship a man who claimed to be the Son of God. That man, Jesus, didn't shy away from teaching what belief in Him—or disbelief—meant. As Jesus explained, whoever believes in Him has eternal life. And those who willingly reject Jesus? They won't see eternal life.

Very clearly, Jesus points to the fact that a decision must be made. Do you choose to believe in Him? Or do you choose not to believe in Him? Your decision affects absolutely everything in this life and what happens after this life.

Jesus, when You walked on earth, people had such polarized opinions of You. The same holds true today. You never were bashful about who You were, though. You are the Son of God. And eternal life comes through You alone. I need to make a decision about You. Do I believe in You? Yes!

HOME SWEET HOME?

The wise woman builds her house, but the foolish tears it down with her own hands.

PROVERBS 14:1 NASB

Homes are places that can welcome and refresh you, but they also can rob you of peace and leave you feeling completely overwhelmed. You may look around and see a huge mess. No matter how hard you try, it seems like you never make any progress. You might look around and focus on everything you need to repair or replace. Or, you might look around and see surroundings you despise. No matter how much you try to appreciate where you live, you truly hate it.

No home is perfect. But regardless of your current home's issues, Proverbs offers a good reminder that wise women build their homes. They find constructive ways to improve their surroundings. They brainstorm possible solutions, then get to work. Foolish women tear their homes down.

The next time you feel overwhelmed with your home, examine your heart and habits. Are you working to build your home up? Or are you intentionally—or unintentionally—tearing it down?

Father, I want to build my home. Please help me make wise choices and live in an insightful way.

ROCKY RELATIONSHIPS

*Finally, all of you, be like-minded, be sympathetic,
love one another, be compassionate and humble. Do
not repay evil with evil or insult with insult. On the
contrary, repay evil with blessing, because to this you
were called so that you may inherit a blessing.*

1 PETER 3:8–9 NIV

Relationships are wonderful—until you experience complications. Sometimes struggles brew for a long time, and other times they'll hit you out of the blue. Sometimes you know exactly what went wrong, and other times you don't have a clue. If you've intentionally or unintentionally stumbled into a conflict with someone else, how can you start to resolve things?

First, pray. Pray for your own attitude and the attitude of the other person. Pray for reconciliation and restoration. Then follow the advice Peter wrote in his letter to believers. Be like-minded. Be sympathetic. Love one another. Be compassionate. Get rid of your pride. Repay evil deeds and insults with blessings. As you do, may you regain the unity you once had.

---

*Father, I'm overwhelmed with grief and frustration
over a particular relationship. Please help me put
my pride aside and respond in love. Please help
me bless even my enemies and become more
sympathetic. I want to be more loving and kind.*

REAPING AND SOWING

*Whoever sows to please their flesh, from the flesh
will reap destruction; whoever sows to please the
Spirit, from the Spirit will reap eternal life.*
GALATIANS 6:8 NIV

Believe it or not, you have a huge influence on what happens in your life. As the apostle Paul wrote to the Galatian church, people reap what they sow.

If you sow only what pleases your flesh, watch out for what you reap—you'll experience destruction. So what pleases your flesh? Behaviors and attitudes that don't please the Spirit of God—like ambition, angry outbursts, drunkenness, envy, hostilities, idolatry, immorality, impurity, jealousy, and strife. When you cultivate those behaviors and attitudes, you'll reap obvious destruction in your life.

But when you sow to please the Spirit of God, you'll reap eternal life. And what's the proof that the Spirit is working in you? You'll experience His love, joy, peace, patience, kindness, goodness, faithfulness, gentleness, and self-control. That's a big difference from life in the flesh. Keep choosing to please the Spirit in what you say and do, and reap the rewards!

---

*Father, as tempting as it might be to try to please
my flesh, I ask You to help me choose to please
You and Your Spirit instead. Sowing to please
You brings amazing, worthwhile results.*

WAIT IN HOPE

We wait in hope for the LORD; he is our help and our shield. In him our hearts rejoice, for we trust in his holy name. May your unfailing love be with us, LORD, even as we put our hope in you.

PSALM 33:20–22 NIV

Depending on what you're waiting for, being patient can feel frustrating. So often, we want to make something happen or hurry along to the next big thing without slowing down and enjoying the process. But waiting can be good.

Since everyone is waiting for something, try to appreciate whatever stage you're in right now. Instead of thinking of possibilities of all that might happen, think about what's good right now. Forget about where you've come from or where you're going. Just focus on now for a moment.

As you focus on right now, think about the trust you've put in the Lord. He's your help. He's your protective shield. You can rejoice and put your hope in Him, because He loves you with a never-failing, never-ending love. Begin to wait in hope for the Lord. Wait for Him to work and move in your life. Wait for His perfect timing and plan.

Father, I can be so impatient at times! As I trust and love You more and more, I pray my patience will grow. I want to wait in hope for You!

KNOWN BY YOUR FRUIT

*"Either assume the tree to be good as well as its
fruit good, or assume the tree to be bad as well as
its fruit bad; for the tree is known by its fruit."*

MATTHEW 12:33 NASB

As hard as it is not to let your attitude, moods, and words
be affected by circumstances, your reactions reveal the fruit
of your life. The heat of the moment will prove who you
really are. Are you producing good fruit? Or do you have
a bumper crop of bad fruit?

When Jesus revealed that you can tell what's in the
heart of a person just by looking at the fruit of her life,
He also revealed that the words you use show what's
inside your heart. Are good things bubbling out of you?
Or do evil things rush to the surface? Only you know
what typically comes out of you when you're provoked. If
good things aren't coming from a good treasure, it's time
to make a change. Start changing your heart so you can
change your fruit for the better.

*Please help me examine my own heart, Lord,
and please work in me so I can bear good fruit.*

GET RID OF IT

*Get rid of all bitterness, rage and anger, brawling
and slander, along with every form of malice.*

EPHESIANS 4:31 NIV

If you've ever spent time decluttering your home, you know some things are easier to get rid of than others. Just like certain belongings need to be purged, certain attitudes and moods do too. Followers of Christ need to get rid of bitterness—*all of it*. Get rid of any rage or anger. Stop brawling. Get rid of all slander. And every form of malice? All your desires to see other people suffer? All your spite and your ill will? Purge it all.

As you get rid of the junk in your personal life, you'll begin to feel freer. You'll experience liberty as you become more Christlike. Get rid of what you don't need in your life so it can be replaced with all the wonderful traits the Lord is ready to add to you.

---

*Father, please help me go on a purging spree! Help me
identify my bitterness, rage, and anger and get rid of it.
Help me find the slander, malice, and brawling tendencies
and send them to the trash. I want to be more like You!*

KEEP ASKING

I remembered my songs in the night. My heart meditated and my spirit asked: "Will the Lord reject forever? Will he never show his favor again? Has his unfailing love vanished forever? Has his promise failed for all time? Has God forgotten to be merciful? Has he in anger withheld his compassion?"

PSALM 77:6–9 NIV

Disappointments in life have a way of sucking joy and optimism from your day, and they keep you tossing and turning at night. As much as you might want to maintain a good attitude or move on, it's hard when grief and concerns overwhelm your thoughts.

When it feels like you can't break free from difficulty, sometimes you're left dealing with big questions. Like the psalmist, it might feel like the Lord is rejecting you. Will He never show His favor again? Has His love vanished? Has His promise failed? Has He forgotten His mercy or withheld His compassion?

God is big enough to handle your questions. Ask Him. Keep pleading for His mercy. Ask for His love and compassion. Beg Him for His favor. Then persistently keep asking Him.

Father, when I'm facing awful situations, sometimes I feel like You're refusing to show me Your love or favor or mercy. Could You please restore Your compassion and kindness to me? Could You please help me experience Your love in a real way?

DON'T FACE IT ALONE

Blessed is the one who perseveres under trial because,
having stood the test, that person will receive the crown
of life that the Lord has promised to those who love him.

JAMES 1:12 NIV

Being able to withstand stress and trials with persistence isn't easy. In fact, needing to endure hardships can leave you feeling powerless and weary. You may not know how to persevere, or you simply might realize your weakness and then doubt you can do it all alone.

The fantastic news is that you don't have to face hardship alone. Of course you can—and should—turn to the Lord for strength and help and guidance. But you can reach out to other people to help too. It's good to talk through situations with trusted friends or counselors. Don't keep your feelings bottled up and try to deal with everything all by yourself. Reach out to someone else and share what's going on in your heart and mind. Open up with your thoughts and feelings. You can ask for advice, or you can just vent. Getting someone else's perspective might be helpful and just what you need.

Father, please show me who I can trust with my
thoughts and feelings. Please help me be vulnerable
and transparent with all that I'm facing.

A SAFE PLACE

The LORD is a refuge for the oppressed,
a stronghold in times of trouble.
PSALM 9:9 NIV

Feeling oppressed is an awful experience that weighs you down. You might be targeted for your beliefs. Something completely beyond your control, like the way you look, might cause others to torment you. You might feel trapped in a current life or health situation with no remedy or relief in sight.

When oppression feels crushing and nothing in this world relieves the tension, remember that your heavenly Father is your safe place. He's a refuge you can run to when you feel trapped or alone. He's your stronghold when you need Him most. When you're facing trouble and you don't know what to do, run to Him in prayer. Give Him your cares and tell Him your concerns. Then step back and trust Him to work so that all things will come together for good. He cares for you and will give you the strength and comfort you need.

Lord, I'm so thankful You're my refuge and
stronghold, because I need You! The trouble
that I'm facing is oppressive. Please help me!

THE LORD IS WITH YOU

And coming in, he said to her, "Greetings, favored one! The Lord is with you." But she was very perplexed at this statement, and was pondering what kind of greeting this was. And the angel said to her, "Do not be afraid, Mary, for you have found favor with God."

LUKE 1:28–30 NASB

As you're living day to day, you don't always feel favored. And you don't always feel like the Lord is with you. The virgin Mary was the same way. As a humble girl, she lived her life without thinking too highly of herself. The Lord knew the beauty of her purity and humility. He knew how much she trusted Him. And He looked on her with favor.

While there's only one Mary in the entirety of history who was favored so much to become the mother of God's Son, God still finds beauty in purity and humility. As you go through life without thinking too highly of yourself, trust Him completely. The Lord is with you. You never know when He might choose to show you and the world how very much He favors you.

Father God, You alone are worthy of my trust and adoration. I don't want to think of myself more highly than I should. I don't want to live in fear either. I want to honor You with my entire life, no matter what You might bring my way.

MAY IT BE DONE

And Mary said, "Behold, the Lord's bond-servant;
may it be done to me according to your word."
And the angel departed from her.
LUKE 1:38 NASB

After the angel Gabriel told Mary that she would conceive and give birth to the Son of the Most High, she was willing to be used by God in this way. As an obedient handmaid of the Lord, she only asked how it would happen because she was a virgin. She didn't need to know every single detail, though. She stepped out in faith, offered herself to be used as the Lord's servant, and was ready to watch the Lord do His work.

Like Mary, you don't need to know all the details of the future. As the Lord's servant, you can pay attention to what the Lord is asking you to do and then respond in trust and willingness. In faith, you can respond like Mary: "I am the Lord's servant; may it be done to me according to Your Word."

Lord, I am Your servant. I offer my life to You. When You
ask me to step out in faith and follow You, I want to
obey. May my life be lived according to Your Word.

THE GIFT OF ENCOURAGEMENT

"And blessed is she who believed that there would be a fulfillment of what had been spoken to her by the Lord."

LUKE 1:45 NASB

Once Mary conceived and was carrying the unborn Jesus, she went to visit her relative Elizabeth. Older and once barren, Elizabeth also knew the miracle of an unexpected pregnancy granted by the Lord. When Mary arrived, Elizabeth's unborn baby, John, leaped in her womb and Elizabeth was filled with the Holy Spirit. She knew Mary was pregnant with the Savior. Elizabeth's reaction was to affirm Mary's faith and belief: "Blessed is she who believed that there would be a fulfillment of what had been spoken to her by the Lord."

When you choose to live by faith but know that could potentially be scary or overwhelming, look for people who will encourage you. Seek those who walk closely with the Lord and will support your steps of faith. With the intercession of other believers, you'll be encouraged to stand against discouragement and doubt.

Father, I'm so glad I don't have to live my life of faith all by myself. Please surround me with other women who love and trust You. Please help me be an encouragement. I pray others will encourage me too.

STRIVING FOR EXCELLENCE

*Whatever you do in word or deed, do everything
in the name of the Lord Jesus, giving thanks
through Him to God the Father.*

COLOSSIANS 3:17 NASB

For women who aim for excellence, there's a huge tendency to feel overwhelmed if they can't measure up to their own standards in everything that they do. When you're committed to doing a good job at work or with your family or in your home, something has to give. As much as you might try to become Wonder Woman and do it all, it's impossible to do everything and do it well.

When you're caught in discouragement or overwhelm because you realize you're neglecting some aspect of your life to focus on another, stop yourself for a moment. What are the commitments in your life you simply must do? What is optional? Once you weigh what you need to do and what you want to do, also stop to consider this: Are you doing everything in the name of the Lord Jesus? The Bible instructs that absolutely everything you do or say needs to be done in His name. Bring glory to Him with the things you do, and give thanks through Him to God the Father.

Lord Jesus, You know my tendency is to try to do too much. Please help me remember to do absolutely everything in Your name and for Your glory.

DEALING WITH LIFE'S CURVEBALLS

*In all labor there is profit, but mere
talk leads only to poverty.*

PROVERBS 14:23 NASB

Life has a funny way of seeming manageable. You think you can get routines and priorities under control—and then, boom! Something happens and throws everything off, so you're left feeling dreadfully off-balance. It happens in relationships and work and scheduling and your home and finances and current events—and just about every single aspect of life.

So what in the world can you do when life throws you a curveball? Proverbs offers sage advice: keep working. There's profit in all labor. Labor means hard work. Instead of only talking about what you *could* or *should* do, get working! Even if it's difficult, keep working. Even if you feel overwhelmed, keep working. As you keep trying and working tiny step by tiny step, you'll make a difference. Slowly, but surely, you can get back into a manageable rhythm.

---

*Father, please help me remember to keep working.
Even when I don't feel like it, I want to work hard.
Please open my eyes to see the really great things
that come from my labor and effort.*

LEARN FROM HIM

"Take my yoke upon you and learn from me, for I am gentle and humble in heart, and you will find rest for your souls. For my yoke is easy and my burden is light."

MATTHEW 11:29–30 NIV

Wouldn't it be amazing to find rest for your soul? In this busy life of going and doing, what if you actually experienced true rest that comes through Christ alone?

Soul rest doesn't come naturally. You can't find it or create it apart from Christ. Jesus said that you can learn from Him. He offers rest, but not to everyone. As British preacher Charles Spurgeon taught, "We must be meek and lowly in heart, otherwise we are totally unfit to be taught by Christ. Empty vessels may be filled; but vessels that are full already can receive no more."*

When you're gentle and humble, you can begin to learn from Jesus. The polar opposite of an overwhelming task, His yoke is easy. He brings rest and refreshment instead of stress and striving. Instead of weighing you down with responsibilities and rules, His burden is light.

Lord Jesus, Your gift of rest is such a beautiful and needed thing. I want to become gentle and humble just like You.

---

*Charles Spurgeon, "The Meek and Lowly One" (sermon, Royal Surrey Gardens, July 31, 1859).

LIGHT

At one time you were darkness, but now you are
light in the Lord. Walk as children of light.

EPHESIANS 5:8 ESV

Our world has been filled with sin ever since Eve ate the forbidden fruit way back in the Garden of Eden. You can expect bad things to happen in this world. And when you add together all the evil and bad in this world of darkness, overwhelm seems obvious.

Once you've experienced Jesus' rescue and you choose to trust Him, He takes you from darkness to light. As the apostle Paul explained, "Now you are light in the Lord." Because you are light living in this dark, dark world, walk as a child of light. Put your past behind you, along with all the habits of your former way of life. You're not tied to this world anymore. Walk and live in the glorious freedom Christ brings you, and shine His light and love to the people around you.

Lord Jesus, thank You for saving me from this dark world.
It's such a gift to become light in You. Please guide my
steps and help me walk as a daughter of Your light.

MY HIDING PLACE

You are my hiding place; you will protect me from
trouble and surround me with songs of deliverance.
PSALM 32:7 NIV

When it feels like you're drowning in overwhelm, it's often hard to know what to do next. You know you're in over your head, but how can you break away from that feeling? What's the first thing to do? Practically speaking, doing a brain dump can be really helpful. Simply take a piece of paper and jot down absolutely any thought that's weighing you down. Need to take care of a lot of random things? Write them all down in one spot. Later you can prioritize how you can handle everything.

Spiritually speaking, though, you can also do a brain dump through prayer. As haphazard as it might seem, tell the Lord every single concern once it comes to mind. After you've done that, rest in Him. You can do any hard work that needs to be done, but you can do it with the peace that Christ alone brings. Remember that the Lord is your hiding place. You can let Him into every aspect of your life, then hide yourself in Him—knowing He's the One who will protect you from trouble and surround you with songs of deliverance.

Father God, I am so glad I can bring all my troubles
and worries to You! Thank You for being
my hiding place. I'm safe in You.

IF YOU MUST SUFFER

For it is better to suffer for doing good,
if that should be God's will, than for doing evil.
1 PETER 3:17 ESV

At some point in life, every person suffers. You might suffer directly, or you might suffer as you walk through a difficult time with someone close to you. Since you know suffering is part of this life, a valid question is why you will suffer. Will you suffer for doing evil and being punished for it? Or will you suffer for doing something good?

The apostle Peter knew the best choice—suffer for doing good. If it's God's will for you to suffer, may you suffer for doing good. The next time you're faced with a decision, Peter's advice will help you consider your response. Will you choose to do good, no matter what the consequence might be?

Father, I'm glad Your will is for me to do good. Please help
me choose good even if it will involve suffering on my part.

A DRAMATIC LIFE

In my alarm I said, "I am cut off from your sight!" Yet you
heard my cry for mercy when I called to you for help.
PSALM 31:22 NIV

Do you tend to get dramatic when you're feeling stressed?
Is it legitimate drama, or do you know that you go over
the top and blow things out of proportion?

King David experienced a huge amount of drama in
his life. He was on the run twice, as his father-in-law and
then his son both sought to kill him. What betrayal! What
danger! This giant slayer killed bears and lions but still
needed to flee for his life and go into hiding. If anyone
had reason to be dramatic, it definitely was David.

When David faced danger at every turn, he gave an
amazing example of what to do: cry out to the Lord. When
David was alarmed, he called out and asked His heavenly
Father for mercy and help. The Lord answered and did give
David mercy and help. He'll give you mercy and help too
in your own dramatic times. Just cry out to Him.

Father, when I need Your mercy and help, I'm thankful I
can rely on You to hear my prayers and answer. Thank You
for listening to me and stepping in with mercy and love.

NOT A SINGLE BIT

Who shall separate us from the love of Christ?
Shall tribulation, or distress, or persecution, or
famine, or nakedness, or danger, or sword?
ROMANS 8:35 ESV

No matter what happens to you in this life, one thing's certain: once you're found in Christ, nothing will separate you from His love. It doesn't matter how you might fumble and stumble and make mistakes. It doesn't matter how much or little you accomplish for Him. You can't do anything to make Him love you more or less. Nothing will separate you from His love.

Tribulation and trials will come, but they can't separate you from Christ and His love and forgiveness. Distress might crash in, but it won't affect His love for you. You might find yourself in an onslaught of persecution. You might starve or be without clothes or a home. You might face serious, life-threatening danger. All that tragedy might happen to you. Yet not a single bit of it will separate you from the love of Christ. Nothing can or will separate you from His love.

Jesus, Your love for me is so much deeper and richer than what I realize. It's such a comfort to know that whatever happens to me in this life, Your love for me will endure forever. Absolutely nothing can separate me from Your love.

NOTHING WILL SEPARATE YOU

For I am sure that neither death nor life, nor angels nor rulers, nor things present nor things to come, nor powers, nor height nor depth, nor anything else in all creation, will be able to separate us from the love of God in Christ Jesus our Lord.

ROMANS 8:38–39 ESV

In his letter to Roman believers, Paul made it clear that no hardship on this earth could separate them from the love of Christ. Not stopping with earthly trials, Paul went on to explain that absolutely nothing could separate a Christ follower from the love of God's Son.

Life can't separate you from Christ's love, and death can't separate you either. No being can separate you from His love—not any earthly ruler nor any angels. Nothing from the past has separated you from His love, and nothing from present times will separate you. No event or thing or person in the future can separate you from His love. Absolutely nothing in creation will be able to separate you from the love of God that's found in Christ Jesus.

To experience His love, you need to know Him. You need to welcome His love by making sure that He's part of your life. Once you've surrendered yourself to Him, bask in His never-ending, unstoppable love.

Christ Jesus my Lord, I'm amazed that Your love for me is unstoppable and never ending. I'm so glad You've let me experience it!

BE ALERT!

The end of all things is near. Therefore be alert and of sober mind so that you may pray. Above all, love each other deeply, because love covers over a multitude of sins.

1 PETER 4:7–8 NIV

When someone else's reaction surprises you or someone doesn't do what you've asked, what then? Dealing with people who act differently than you expect can be disappointing and discouraging. If you have the same complaints or ask for the same corrections over and over again, it's natural to feel like a disheartened hamster on a wheel. You may need to use a lot of energy but feel like you're getting absolutely nowhere. In those times of frustration, try to keep life in perspective.

Now, more than ever before, the end of all things is near. Because of this, we need to keep loving the people in our lives, because love covers sin. It helps us see things from a healthy perspective instead of in a critical, fault-finding way. And since the end is coming soon, it's good to be alert to what's happening. When you feel frustrated or fearful, avoid panicking and pouting. Instead, pray.

Lord Jesus, the day of Your return is coming soon. Please help me keep this in mind as I deal with the frustrations of this life. I want to obey You and love others deeply.

GOD'S APPROVAL

*Am I now trying to win the approval of human beings,
or of God? Or am I trying to please people? If I were still
trying to please people, I would not be a servant of Christ.*

GALATIANS 1:10 NIV

Being a people pleaser can add so much unnecessary stress
and pressure to your life. Instead of experiencing peace by
winning the unchangeable approval of God, when you try
to please people you get caught in a never-ending game of
trying to figure out what someone else prefers. You never
know when opinions and tastes may change—you're truly
at the whim of an ever-evolving judge.

Servants of Christ don't seek to please people. The
apostle Paul knew this, and he encouraged believers to try
to please the Lord. Try to win God's approval. You can do
this by forgetting about people around you and focusing
on the One you want to serve.

---

*Father God, I want to please You and You
alone. I want to keep my focus on winning Your
approval and serving You faithfully all my days.*

LISTEN

Listen to my words, LORD, consider my sighing.
Listen to the sound of my cry for help, my
King and my God, for to You I pray.
PSALM 5:1–2 NASB

How many times have you started talking to someone, only to realize they weren't listening to you at all? It's pretty frustrating to know that even if you feel like you have something important to say, no one stops to listen.

One of God's many amazingly fantastic qualities is that He listens to you all the time. He never gets bored or tunes you out. When you're concerned or overwhelmed or you feel like you're at your wit's end, He's there to consider your sighing. The Lord of hosts listens to the sound of your cry for help. The King of all kings listens to your prayers. Instead of needing to approach a messenger who will give Him your request, you can approach His throne of grace with confidence.

My King and my God, thank You for listening to me and
my cries for help. Thank You for considering my sighing.
I'm so thankful I can pray to You and know You listen.

SALTY

"You are the salt of the earth. But if the salt loses its saltiness, how can it be made salty again? It is no longer good for anything, except to be thrown out and trampled underfoot."

MATTHEW 5:13 NIV

No matter what may be going on in your life right now, if you're a believer, you're called to be light in this dark world. You're salt here on earth too. As salt, you can add flavor to a bland culture. You can help preserve and slow the rot and decay of this world. And just like salt helps your body function properly, salt is essential for the body of Christ.

But what happens if you're not as salty as you once were? Salt that loses its saltiness is ineffective and useless. When it's not helpful, it's not good for anything except the garbage. Use this time in your life to be salty. If you know you've lost some of your original saltiness, return to your love for Christ. Don't be afraid to stand out in this world and stand up for your faith. Be the salt you're meant to be!

Father, no matter how inspired or energized I might feel, please help me be salty. I want to point the world to You!

EXPOSING THE DARKNESS

*Have nothing to do with the fruitless deeds of
darkness, but rather expose them. It is shameful even
to mention what the disobedient do in secret. But
everything exposed by the light becomes visible—and
everything that is illuminated becomes a light.*

EPHESIANS 5:11–13 NIV

Believers of Christ are lights in this dark world, and it's
important to stay light. What's the opposite of light?
Darkness. And what does light drive away? Darkness.
Because light and darkness are opposites, the apostle Paul
instructed the Ephesian church to expose the darkness.

If you notice darkness around you, it might make you
feel overwhelmed. Like being trapped in a room without
any light, discovering darkness in this world can be scary.
But just like light drives darkness away, believers are called
to expose the deeds of darkness. Shine some light on
shameful disobedience so others are warned. Exposing
the darkness might seem impossible, like it's a huge task
you never can conquer. But keep being the light. Let your
light shine in this dark world.

*Father, it feels like my little light for You is so tiny in this big,
dark world. But light makes a difference. It's visible. Please fill
me with courage to stand up and be a light in the darkness.*

WHY SHOULD I FEAR?

Why should I fear when evil days come, when
wicked deceivers surround me—those who trust
in their wealth and boast of their great riches?

PSALM 49:5–6 NIV

Fear and overwhelm often go hand in hand in a chicken-and-the-egg kind of way. What came first? The fear? Or the overwhelm?

When you find yourself in the middle of a cycle of fear, it's time to break free. Why should you fear? Even if you're in the middle of evil days surrounded by wicked deceivers, you don't have to fear. God will redeem your life. He has a purpose and a plan, and He will work it out.

Because the Lord of the universe is working all things together for good to those who love Him and are called according to His purpose (Romans 8:28), you don't have to worry. You don't have to feel overwhelmed with fear.

Father, I'm so thankful I don't have to fear evil days or
evil people. What a gift You've given me. Thank You
for freedom and peace that come through You!

LISTENING VS. SPEAKING

My dear brothers and sisters, take note of this:
Everyone should be quick to listen, slow to speak and
slow to become angry, because human anger does
not produce the righteousness that God desires.

JAMES 1:19–20 NIV

Words have a way of spilling out of your mouth if you're not careful. And if you're feeling overwhelmed and upset? There's a greater chance that you might say something you don't intend to say.

No matter how stressed you might feel, it's best to follow biblical advice before opening your mouth. Be quick to listen. Process what's being said. Be slow to speak. Don't say the first thing that comes to mind. Instead, mull over your words first. And be slow to become angry. Instead of flying off the handle at any little annoyance, let gentleness rule. As much as you may feel that your anger is justified, it will never produce the kind of righteousness that pleases the Lord.

Father, please help me watch what I say! Put a guard
over my mouth if necessary. I want to become quick
to listen and slow to speak, but I need Your help.

YOUR HELPER

*Do not hide your face from me, do not turn your servant
away in anger; you have been my helper. Do not reject
me or forsake me, God my Savior. Though my father
and mother forsake me, the LORD will receive me.*

PSALM 27:9–10 NIV

In his poetry, King David acknowledged that God, his
Savior, had been his helper. Even in hard times when
everyone else seemed to abandon David, he knew God
was always on his side. And he knew the Holy Spirit was
helping him. As Psalm 51:11 reveals, David asked the
Lord not to take the Holy Spirit away from him.

The Holy Spirit is part of believers' lives as a
helper—that's one of His roles. During Jesus' life on earth,
He promised He would ask the Father to give the Spirit
as a helper who would never leave. The Holy Spirit would
teach believers all things and remind them of what Christ
taught. As long as you're in Christ, you have the Holy
Spirit as your own helper. He'll help you navigate through
life and help you when you need Him most.

*God my Savior, thank You for Your wonderful gift of
the Holy Spirit. Thank You for the way He helps me!*

THE FRUIT OF DISCIPLINE

*For the moment all discipline seems painful rather
than pleasant, but later it yields the peaceful fruit of
righteousness to those who have been trained by it.*

HEBREWS 12:11 ESV

Discipline is never enjoyable. And that's not just behavioral discipline either. Other kinds of discipline are hard too. It's hard to be disciplined in the way you eat or exercise. Sticking to a disciplined schedule or routine can seem tricky when you skip things you'd like to do so you can do what you need to do.

Even if it's hard, discipline is a really good thing. Over time, all the discipline in your life becomes a beautiful thing. Your discipline is a lot like a fruit tree—you plant it, nurture it, and make sure you get rid of the weeds that crop up. Over time, that tree will bear good fruit. That good fruit would be impossible without a gardener's watchful eye and regular care. In your own life, all your discipline will develop into the wonderful fruit of righteousness. You'll enjoy all the benefits of right living when you choose to stick to a disciplined life.

---

*Father, I know I should seek discipline in my life, but
I don't always enjoy it. Even if it seems difficult to
add it to my life or stick with it, please help me do it.
Through Your power, I want to live a life of discipline!*

THE WAITING GAME

The Lord is good to those who wait for him, to the soul who seeks him. It is good that one should wait quietly for the salvation of the Lord.

LAMENTATIONS 3:25–26 ESV

Every person goes through different seasons of life. When you discover you have more free time than you're used to having, what should you do? If you try to fill your time with absolutely everything you've ever wanted to attempt, you might start to feel overwhelmed. How can you choose your pursuits wisely?

Before jumping into a bunch of commitments only to later realize you've overcommitted yourself, first seek wisdom from the Lord. Prayerfully ask Him for guidance and direction, and then spend time in His Word as you wait for Him. Even if you're prone to jump right in and get busy, wait. Is this difficult? You bet. Could it take longer than you expect? Yes! But as you patiently and quietly wait for the Lord, He'll open up doors in a surprising way. Don't be afraid to confidently walk into the plans He has for you.

Father God, I choose to wait for Your guidance and direction. Please show me what's best for right now. I'm excited to discover the opportunities You'll bring into my life! Help me grow in patience as I wait for You.

WALKING THROUGH TRIALS

Beloved, do not be surprised at the fiery trial when it comes upon you to test you, as though something strange were happening to you. But rejoice insofar as you share Christ's sufferings, that you may also rejoice and be glad when his glory is revealed.

1 PETER 4:12–13 ESV

Tragedies strike when you least expect it, leaving you reeling with disappointment and grief. When you're left picking up the pieces of a life shattered by ugly circumstances, what do you do?

First, as shocking as your situation might seem, don't be surprised. Trials and tragedies are part of this life. As you suffer, you have a chance to endure and grow. Will it be easy? Of course not. But you can become a stronger person and develop faith as you turn to the Lord for strength and guidance.

Just as Christ faced suffering He didn't deserve, you may face suffering you don't deserve as well. When you do, rejoice that His glory can be revealed to you and through you in your suffering. Not only will you identify with Christ even more, but you'll also get a firsthand view of the way He's at work in your situation.

Lord Jesus, suffering seems so wrong and painful. You, of all people, know that. Please help me remember that as devastated as I might feel right now, You can work something beautiful out of this experience, and for that I'm grateful.

WHO ARE YOU?

Whatever happens, conduct yourselves in a manner
worthy of the gospel of Christ. Then, whether I come
and see you or only hear about you in my absence,
I will know that you stand firm in the one Spirit,
striving together as one for the faith of the gospel.

PHILIPPIANS 1:27 NIV

Trying times have a way of showing your true grit. Anyone can put on a happy face and seem like a good, kind person when all is going smoothly in life. But once struggles begin? That's another story.

Who are you when times get tough? Do you buckle under pressure? Do you panic out of fear? Or do you stay pretty much unchanged? Do you conduct yourself in a manner that's worthy of the Gospel of Christ?

When your character stays the same regardless of what's going on in life, you show yourself and the world that you stand firm in your relationship with Christ. If you're content with who you are when you face trying times, keep up your faithful walk of life! But if you'd like to change, it's not too late. Get closer to the Lord in the everyday parts of life by praying as well as studying the Bible, and develop an unshakable, unchangeable faith.

Lord Jesus, I want my faith in You to shine all the time—
in both good and bad times. Please help me live every
aspect of my life in a manner worthy of Your Gospel.

SATISFIED

*A person will be satisfied with good by
the fruit of his words, and the deeds of
a person's hands will return to him.*

Proverbs 12:14 NASB

Take a moment to look around your home. Are you satisfied with what you see? Are you satisfied by the way you feel? Or frustrated? As Proverbs promises, the work of your hands will return to you. If you diligently work around your home, you'll notice a difference. And if you choose to skip any housework, you'll notice that too.

When you consider the attitudes in your home, are you pleased? Or frustrated? While you certainly can't control someone else's moods and feelings, you can work on your own. Are you cultivating peace with your words and attitudes? Or are you stirring up bitterness and strife? When your words are fruitful, you'll be satisfied with the good that comes from them.

Always remember, when you go the sometimes difficult extra mile of choosing diligence and kindness, you'll reap rewards and satisfaction.

*Father, even and especially when I don't feel like
it, please help me choose kindness with others.
Please give me energy to do the hard work.*

GIVING LIGHT

"You are the light of the world. A city set on a hill cannot be hidden; nor do people light a lamp and put it under a basket, but on the lampstand, and it gives light to all who are in the house."

MATTHEW 5:14–15 NASB

At times, the darkness and sin in this world feel so oppressive. It's obvious that there's an evil resistance to all that is good and holy. Yet believers aren't called to cave in to the darkness. We shouldn't throw up our hands in surrender, thinking all hope is gone.

All hope is *not* gone. If you know Jesus Christ and have asked Him to take over as Lord of your life and to save you from all your shortcomings and sins, you have great hope. Your hope in Christ lights up your life. And your life can light up this world.

Imagine looking out of an airplane in the dark of night. You may not be able to see the ground, but you can see lights. You might see one light here and one light there, but when you approach a city, the entire sky is aglow with light. Just like those lights on a dark night, let your light for Christ shine brightly.

Lord Jesus, it's amazing that Your light shines through me in this darkened world. Please help me boldly bring the light of Your truth into the world around me.

LET YOUR LIGHT SHINE

"In the same way, let your light shine before others,
that they may see your good deeds and
glorify your Father in heaven."

MATTHEW 5:16 NIV

Believing and trusting in Christ makes you light up in such a way that's noticeable to others around you. This light is something you can't extinguish, and no one else can either. It's just there.

You shouldn't try to hide this special light in order to fit into the world. Instead, let your light shine before all the people around you. It's a good thing you're different! Whatever situation you find yourself in, let your light drive away the darkness of this world. Your light might be something as simple as showing kindness to someone you meet. Or it could be as deep as telling someone how Jesus changed your life.

As you let your light shine brightly, others will notice the good that you do. They'll notice you're different. And they'll glorify God because of you.

Father, thank You for this light of mine.
I want to let it shine in this dark world!

OVERWHELMED BY LONELINESS

*Behold, the eye of the L*ORD *is on those who fear Him,*
on those who wait for His faithfulness, to rescue their
soul from death and to keep them alive in famine.

PSALM 33:18–19 NASB

Living all by yourself in this world can leave you feeling overwhelmed with loneliness. As humans, we were created for connection and interactions. It can take a long time to get used to being a Lone Ranger.

Even if you feel that the solitude you're facing is just too much to handle and you long for someone else, remember that you're not truly alone. Psalm 33 reveals that if you fear the Lord and wait for His faithfulness, His eye is on you. He sees and knows what you're experiencing. He is ready to rescue you and keep you alive in famine— even in a famine of close relationships.

Lord, thank You for watching out for me and always,
always being there for me. You know my heart.
You know my pain and the way I long for someone
to care for me. Please comfort me with Your love
and help me find my contentment in You.

THE HARDNESS OF HARDSHIPS

*Endure hardship as discipline; God is treating you
as his children. For what children are not disciplined
by their father? If you are not disciplined—and
everyone undergoes discipline—then you are not
legitimate, not true sons and daughters at all.*

HEBREWS 12:7–8 NIV

If relentless waves of hardship have been crashing in until you doubt you can take any more, you can be sure that your endurance is growing. Whether you like it or not, endurance is a good trait of spiritual maturity. It's not easy to come by, but it's necessary for growth.

Since God allows all things to happen, He knows about your hardship—and He has let it be part of your life.

Why would a loving God allow such a thing? True love involves watching someone grow and mature to become a better person. All of that growth and maturity doesn't happen naturally. That's where hardship enters the picture. The Lord chooses to discipline you through hardships as a way to help your endurance and strength grow. As He does this for you, it's proof that you're really His daughter. He loves you so much. He wants to watch you bloom and grow, even if the growing process takes a lot more out of you than you'd prefer.

---

*Father, I know I should welcome endurance as a way to grow
into a more complete woman. But it's so hard! Even if I don't
prefer Your discipline, please have Your way in my life.*

PEACE

*In peace I will both lie down and sleep; for you
alone, O LORD, make me dwell in safety.*

PSALM 4:8 ESV

In the middle of an overwhelmed life, thoughts have a
way of rushing through your mind as you try to fall asleep
at night. Left to your own pondering and imagination,
your thoughts may not slow down for hours. So what's
an effective solution? You could keep a pad of paper and
pen beside your bed to jot down your thoughts as you toss
and turn at night.

Or you could attempt to fall asleep by talking to the
Lord. Try thinking of everything that happened in your
day that you're thankful for—both little and big things.
Invite Him into the thoughts that are keeping you awake. If
you've been upset by something, call out to Him and share
every detail. Tell Him your joys and concerns. Ponder who
you're talking with and praise His holy name. Consider
His wonderful character traits.

As you set your mind on your heavenly Father, you'll
be able to lie down and sleep in peace. He's the One who
will keep you dwelling in safety.

*Father, thank You for keeping me safe as I sleep.
I pray I'll put my anxious thoughts behind me.
Help me concentrate on You and rest.*

A FRUITFUL LIFE

*"I am the vine; you are the branches. If you
remain in me and I in you, you will bear much
fruit; apart from me you can do nothing."*

JOHN 15:5 NIV

Have you ever watched a dead tree branch that's lying on the ground end up sprouting leaves and growing fruit? You haven't observed this, because it's impossible. Unless a branch is attached to a tree, it's not thriving. It's impossible for a dead branch to bear fruit.

In the same way, it's impossible for you to sprout and bloom and grow or produce any kind of fruit apart from Christ. When you're connected to Him, He's the One to nourish and empower you. Left to your own strength and ability, you can only do so much. (Or truly, so little.) But tap into your Savior's power and strength? Who knows what He'll do through you!

One thing's for sure: if you're in Christ—meaning you're trusting in Him to save you and work through you—there's no telling what He'll grow and produce through your surrendered life.

Lord Jesus, I'm so relieved to know I don't have to try to force things to happen on my own. What a gift it is to only need to remain in You and watch You work through me.

CALM DOWN

*A hot-tempered person stirs up conflict,
but the one who is patient calms a quarrel.*
PROVERBS 15:18 NIV

Do you know what ignites a tense situation into a flaming, disastrous mess? Hot tempers. While anger is not sinful—it's simply one of many emotions everyone experiences—acting out in anger creates huge problems.

When you're in the middle of a conflict and don't want to see it blow up into an all-out battle, watch your temper! It might mean that you need to swallow your pride and hold your tongue, but you should pray for wisdom in how to proceed. With great patience and discernment, try to calm yourself down first. Once you've done that, respond with patience and humility. Choose a loving, kind response. If you need to fake it until you truly feel loving or kind, then fake it. But choose a gentle response instead of an angry one. Calm a quarrel instead of instigating one. Become a peacemaker.

Father, it's so hard to not react in anger, especially when others provoke me. Please help me choose kindness and love. Please help me live a life of patience and gentleness.

HIS NAMESAKE

*However, if you suffer as a Christian, do not be
ashamed, but praise God that you bear that name.*

1 PETER 4:16 NIV

If you pay attention to current events or popular opinion, you've probably noticed that Christians are an unpopular bunch in the world's eyes. For a variety of reasons, nonbelievers have no problem listing off exactly how they feel about Christians.

This is nothing new. Ever since Christ was persecuted and killed, His believers have faced opposition. But should opposition and persecution persuade you to give up your faith in Christ? By all means, no!

What this does mean is that you can expect persecution. You can expect disagreements and misunderstanding. As you face opposition, you don't have to be ashamed. Instead, you can praise God that you bear the name of Christ. You can praise God that you're learning to identify with Christ through suffering. It won't be easy, but it's not the end of the world. You have eternity to anticipate.

---

*Father, suffering is never easy or enjoyable. But if I must suffer
for the sake of You, please help me take it in stride. Please
open my eyes to the way I'm sharing in Christ's sufferings.*

A WORKING WOMAN

Are you so foolish? Having begun by the Spirit,
are you now being perfected by the flesh?
GALATIANS 3:3 ESV

If you're a go-getting, do-it-yourself woman, it can be really tough to let things go. When you realize you can't do a single thing to win Christ's approval or to make Him love you more, it can be both a relief and a bit of a letdown. You don't have to do anything to earn your salvation? That's a huge perspective shift.

Just like you can't work your way to heaven, once you've been saved by the grace of God, you can't work to improve or perfect your spiritual worth. Any growth comes from the Spirit of God working in you. You don't have to wear yourself out trying to be more. You're free from needing to think of ways to perfect your faith. God's grace abundantly changes your eternity, and it changes your life here on earth. Just as He alone saves, He also works out His will in the life of every believer. Trust in Him and His powerful process.

Father, thank You that I don't have to work to save myself
or make myself better. I want to trust You completely
and keep my eyes on You as You work in my life.

TRUST IN HIM

Commit your way to the LORD;
trust in him, and he will act.
PSALM 37:5 ESV

Even though the Lord is the One at work in you to bring you to greater spiritual maturity, it's not like you get to sit on the sidelines for the entire process. After all, you're still living life. You haven't turned into a mindless zombie without a will.

You might wonder where the sweet spot is. You don't want to run ahead and try to make things happen on your own. You also don't want to kick back and relax as you watch Him work everything out. Somehow, you have to find a place where the Lord is leading and guiding and you're listening and responding in obedience.

Part of the secret is committing your way to the Lord. Trust Him completely. Know He will act, and wait for Him. Then be ready to be obedient. If He's clearly guiding you to do something, follow His lead. If He's clearly shutting a door, you can give yourself time to be disappointed, but don't try to force things to happen. This can be a bit of a dance as you learn how to let go and follow God's lead, but it gets easier the more you obey your Father.

Father God, I commit my way to You! I trust You
completely! Please help me follow You and Your ways.

MAKING THINGS RIGHT

"If you are offering your gift at the altar and there remember that your brother has something against you, leave your gift there before the altar and go. First be reconciled to your brother, and then come and offer your gift."

MATTHEW 5:23–24 ESV

Living in conflict is never easy. When you know in your heart of hearts that there's a rift between you and another person, you feel discomfort. Just like *you* know when you're not unified with someone else, the Lord knows too. As the champion for unity, He wants to make sure you settle matters with others.

Jesus taught that if you have a conflict with someone else, you need to mend it before offering anything to the Lord. Reconciliation really is that important. Granted, seeking reconciliation may not be easy or comfortable, but it is necessary.

Today, consider the relationships in your life. Do you need to be reconciled with anyone in particular?

Father, it's not always easy to remember that unity is such a big deal to You. Please help me make the uncomfortable first step of reconciliation.

MAKING THE MOST OF YOUR TIME

So then, be careful how you walk, not as unwise people but as wise, making the most of your time, because the days are evil.

EPHESIANS 5:15–16 NASB

So much of overwhelm is tied up with time. If only you had enough time to do all the things you want or need to do, you wouldn't feel so overwhelmed!

Time is at a premium for almost everyone. We're all given the same twenty-four-hour days and seven-day weeks. So how can you fit all of your life into those increments of time? You can begin to maximize your time by considering what you're doing. How much time do you tend to waste every day? What's the best use of your time? What do you truly need to get done? What would you like to get done but it's just not that important? Who do you need to spend time with?

As you figure out your priorities, it's wise to follow the advice of the apostle Paul, who said it's a good thing to be careful how you walk—how you live your life. Make the most of your time, whatever that might look like for you. In doing so, you'll live as a wise woman!

Father, please show me what I need to prioritize in my schedule and what I need to boldly eliminate. I want to be wise and make the most of my time!

STILLNESS

"Be still, and know that I am God. I will be exalted among the nations, I will be exalted in the earth!"

PSALM 46:10 ESV

For many women, busyness and striving and flitting from one thing to the next and always having some kind of background noise has become such a normal part of life. But what if all the demands for your time and energy are what drain your peace and joy?

All the way back in the Psalms, God asked His followers to be still and know that He is God. That means you can stop striving and know He will be exalted over all. Since He is the Lord of all, you don't have to spend so much time pushing yourself and working hard and trying to make life happen. Relax. It's okay! He is God. As frenzied as you might feel, slow down and enjoy this life He's given you. He knows all that's going on and all that will happen. Everything's under His control. Stop your striving and know that He is God.

Father God, Maker of heaven and earth, I praise You! You are good, and Your mercy and love endure forever. I exalt Your holy name. Because You are God, I can stop my striving. I want to enjoy You in the stillness today.

PARENTAL PEACE

Peacemakers who sow in peace
reap a harvest of righteousness.
JAMES 3:18 NIV

If you're a mom of more than one child, no one needs to tell you that whether you like it or not, you have to develop peacemaking skills. Often the peacemaker in your family, you not only need to hear sibling squabbles and tattletales, but you also need to respond wisely to conflicts. How serious is the issue? Has this behavior happened before, or is it new to your family? Is a punishment necessary? If so, what kind?

As you discover the needs of your children and figure out how to respond appropriately, you become a peace-maker. The great news is that as long as you're acting as the peacemaker and encouraging peace in your home, you'll eventually enjoy a harvest of righteousness. Righteousness just for keeping the peace in your home? That's a fantastic return on your investment of time, thought, and initiative.

Father, having a quiet, controlled home isn't my only goal when raising my children. Please help me impart life lessons to them. Please help me effectively teach them how to become great humans who love and honor You while respecting other people.

THE ANGUISH OF OVERWHELM

*Have mercy on me, LORD, for I am faint; heal me,
LORD, for my bones are in agony. My soul is in
deep anguish. How long, LORD, how long?*

PSALM 6:2–3 NIV

Feeling perpetually overwhelmed directly affects the way you feel and think. As *Harvard Business Review* reported, "The cognitive impact of feeling perpetually overwhelmed can range from mental slowness, forgetfulness, confusion, difficulty concentrating or thinking logically, to a racing mind or an impaired ability to problem solve. When we have too many demands on our thinking over an extended period of time, cognitive fatigue can also happen, making us more prone to distractions and our thinking less agile."*

You might relate to feeling faint, as Psalm 6 describes. Your bones might ache in agony, and your soul might feel tormented in deep anguish. How can you deal with this kind of overwhelm? First, ask the Lord for His mercy and discernment. He may step in to heal you, or He may give you insight into what demands are necessary and what demands are unnecessary. Follow His lead and bravely cut out what needs to be eliminated. As you do, watch how your overwhelm eases.

---

*Have mercy on me, Lord! I feel faint and anguished
over all my perpetual overwhelm. Please help
me learn to say no to all that's unnecessary.*

*Rebecca Zucker, "How to Deal with Constantly Feeling Overwhelmed," *Harvard Business Review*, October 2019.

TEMPTED

For we do not have a high priest who cannot sympathize
with our weaknesses, but One who has been tempted
in all things just as we are, yet without sin.

HEBREWS 4:15 NASB

Realizing Christ has been tempted in all things can be a huge comfort to believers. Not only does He understand our weaknesses; but in our weaknesses, He also sympathizes with us.

Because Jesus has experienced the power of temptation and the weakness of human willpower, you can bring absolutely any of your concerns to Him. In prayer, tell Him about your struggles. Ask Him to help you with whatever temptations you're facing. When you feel overwhelmed by tempting urges, cry out to Him. Ask for His help. He's your Savior and your friend. He can help you deal with any temptation you face.

Lord Jesus, You are amazing. It's such a comfort to know that You understand me completely. You know how powerful temptation is. Please help me resist sinning against You.

DRAW NEAR

*Let us then with confidence draw near to the
throne of grace, that we may receive mercy
and find grace to help in time of need.*

HEBREWS 4:16 ESV

When you're facing a time of need, deep down you know
you're unable to do things in your own power or strength.
How do you deal with your feelings of inadequacy? How
do you manage to keep going?

The author of Hebrews offered a clear-cut solution
for followers of Christ: draw near to the throne of grace.
Forget about doing it sheepishly or with shame, though.
You need to draw near with confidence. It's okay that you
need help. It's okay that you're needy. As a human, you
have weaknesses and imperfections.

As your Creator, the Lord knows all of this, and He's
ready to step in and help you. The divine help He will give
you is filled with mercy and grace. These gifts may seem
different from what you think you need, but they're a
perfect fit. And they're yours once you draw near to your
heavenly Father's throne of grace.

---

*Father, I humbly ask You for help! I can't do things
on my own, and I know it. Could You please
pour out Your mercy and grace in my life?*

ALL IN

Whoever follows His word, in him the love of God has truly been perfected. By this we know that we are in Him: the one who says that he remains in Him ought, himself also, walk just as He walked.

1 JOHN 2:5–6 NASB

As a believer in Christ, if you ever wonder how you should live—what decisions you should make, how you should treat others, how you should behave in your daily life—the answer is a simple one: follow God's Word. Of course, choosing obedience may not always feel simple if you're tempted to go your own way and do your own thing. But knowing what to do is simple because it's spelled out in the Bible.

John specified that when you obey God and His Word, it proves that God's love has been perfected in you. When you walk like Jesus walked and live by the same principles as He did, you'll demonstrate that you truly have a relationship with Him.

If you're in the middle of a decision-making process and know what choice would glorify God but you're just not quite sure you can actually commit to it, go all in. Follow His Word! Walk just as He walked!

Lord Jesus, thank You for demonstrating how Your followers should live. I want to follow Your Word. I want God's love to be perfected in me! I want to walk just as You walked.

FOLLOW HIS LEAD

Therefore, as you have received Christ Jesus the Lord, so walk in Him, having been firmly rooted and now being built up in Him and established in your faith, just as you were instructed, and overflowing with gratitude.

COLOSSIANS 2:6–7 NASB

Regardless of what you're facing in life—maybe you're currently in a calm, sweet spot or you're in the middle of a raging, life-altering storm—you're called to live in a particular way if you've received Christ Jesus as Lord. If you've been firmly rooted in your faith, you're currently being built up in Him. Your faith is being established, both in easy times and hard ones.

As your faith in Him is established, make sure you gratefully give Him thanks for all that He's doing in your heart and life. Whether the life you're living seems filled with blessings or one difficulty after another, walk in Him. Follow His lead. Watch the way He builds and develops your faith and trust in Him.

Lord Jesus, my life is infinitely better because I've received You. No matter what I face in this life, I pray my faith will remain firmly grounded in You. I trust You completely as You build up my faith even in times of difficulty. I'm so thankful for You and what You're doing in my life!

WORKING YOUR PLANS

*Plans fail for lack of counsel, but with
many advisers they succeed.*
PROVERBS 15:22 NIV

So much of everyday life is made easier with planning. If you take the time to consider what's needed, make plans, and then work your plans, your time and energy is freed up so you can do other things.

Redundant daily chores around your home or figuring out and preparing daily meals might seem like thankless, never-ending tasks, but with a little planning, the process will be easier. If you don't feel like you're a good enough cook to brainstorm tasty, healthy dinners to serve every day, the good news is you can consult people who have a passion for meal planning. The same goes for tackling chores around your home. If you don't know what to do, learn from someone else who does.

While you certainly can ask people you respect in your own life, you also can get ideas from books or take advantage of online resources. As the book of Proverbs wisely says, "plans fail for lack of counsel." If you try to do absolutely everything on your own without asking advice from anyone else, chances are your process will be a lot trickier and messier. Instead, ask for help. Take advice and watch your plans succeed.

---

*Father, I'm relieved that I don't need to be
an expert in everything. Please bring the right
counselors into my life with just the advice I need.*

FEELING BURDENED?

*"Come to me, all you who are weary and
burdened, and I will give you rest."*

MATTHEW 11:28 NIV

Taking time to rest is often forgotten when you're feeling overwhelmed by burdens. After all, how can you get everything done if you're resting? And how can you begin to deal with the emotional baggage if you set it to the side and take a break?

Jesus offered the most amazing, appealing gift to any woman dealing with overwhelm: Come to Him. He will give you rest.

You're weary. You're burdened. But the fantastic news is you don't have to get your act together to come to Him. You don't have to wait until you're filled with energy and cheerfulness. You don't need to solve your problems first. You don't need to work through your burdens ahead of time. Simply come to Him.

Come in your weariness. Come with your burdens. Lay them down at His feet, and enjoy the rest that only He can give. Come to Jesus and rest in Him.

---

*Lord Jesus, I love and adore You. I worship You as Lord
of all. Thank You for calling me to Yourself. Thank You
for offering Your beautiful, refreshing gift of rest.*

THE GIFT OF FORGIVENESS

*Be kind and compassionate to one another, forgiving
each other, just as in Christ God forgave you.*

EPHESIANS 4:32 NIV

Forgiveness takes a huge amount of humility. Humbly coming before someone to ask for forgiveness requires swallowing your pride to do what's right. And offering forgiveness to someone who's wronged you takes humility and kindness and compassion.

If you ever find yourself in a situation where you know you've been wronged and you know you need to offer forgiveness but you know you just don't want to, an easy motivator is to remember how much you've been forgiven. No one is perfect. You've had to apologize to and seek forgiveness from people in your life, and you've definitely needed forgiveness from Christ.

The Lord of the universe forgives you when you recognize and repent of your sin. He doesn't have to do this. He could hold a grudge. He could demand that you're held to a higher standard. But time after time He offers you forgiveness. In the same way, be willing to forgive others in your life. Since you've been forgiven of much, you can forgive much.

---

*Jesus, thank You for Your forgiveness! It's undeserved,
and I need it so much more often than I'd like to
admit. But I'm so grateful for it. Please help me show
the same kind, compassionate forgiveness to others.*

THE LORD IS GOOD!

*Taste and see that the LORD is good; blessed
is the one who takes refuge in him.*

PSALM 34:8 NIV

Look all around you and you'll see evidence of the Lord's goodness. You can see His goodness in the faces and lives of people. You can see it in the beauty and wonder of nature. You can see it in the way your life circumstances point directly to His will and way.

His goodness is a fantastic gift everyone in the world enjoys. But many people choose to take His goodness for granted and ignore the Giver of all good gifts.

Instead of looking past the Lord, you can choose to acknowledge and worship Him. Instead of clinging to your own ability, you can choose to place all your trust in Him and surrender yourself to Him. As you do, you take refuge in Him. He becomes your safe place and comforting haven. He becomes your rescue. As you make that choice, He fills your life with blessings even greater and richer than the goodness He extends to everyone.

---

*Father God, You are Lord of all! I want You to be
Lord of my heart. Thank You for Your goodness. I
praise You that You are a safe place and refuge I
can run to anytime. I trust You completely!*

THE LORD AND HIS CHURCH

Now I know that the LORD saves his anointed;
he will answer him from his holy heaven
with the saving might of his right hand.

PSALM 20:6 ESV

Churches seem like they should be ideal places—it's where the body of Christ meets to worship and serve their Savior. Yet how often do church members feel overwhelmed by conflicts or disagreements or serving to the point of overcommitment?

As challenging as it is to set aside worldly needs and opinions and focus on the Lord regarding church matters, it's crucial. The Lord is the One who saves with might and undeserved mercy and grace. The Lord is the One who answers. The Lord is the One who wills and works in the lives of His believers and His church.

The next time you're tempted to make church all about yourself, turn your eyes to Jesus, the Author and Perfecter of your faith. How can you make your time at church all about Him?

Lord, You are good! Your mercy endures forever. Thank You for calling me to be part of Your church. Please use me in Your body of believers to point others to You.

WHERE'S YOUR TRUST?

*Some trust in chariots and some in horses, but
we trust in the name of the LORD our God. They
collapse and fall, but we rise and stand upright.*

PSALM 20:7–8 ESV

For thousands of years, people have fallen into the trap of
thinking rulers and governments can save them and make
everything in life better. But the fact of the matter is that
rulers can only govern people—they can't save them. The
same goes for the comforts of this world. You may think
your life will be better if you have a certain possession or
live in a certain place, but those are just passing fancies.

If you're honest with yourself and realize you're trusting in something this world offers, it's time to reconsider.
Will you continue to place your trust in people or things
of this world?

Eventually everything in this world will collapse and
fall; this has been happening since creation. When you
stop trusting in temporal things and begin completely
trusting in the eternal God, your entire perspective shifts.
Trusting in the Lord will give you strength to rise and
stand upright. Trusting in the Lord offers you hope and
a promise for your future like nothing else.

---

*Oh Lord my God, please help me not cave into the
pressures of this world. I don't want to trust in
other people or authorities or my treasures.
I want to trust in You completely!*

HONOR AND THANKS

For although they knew God, they did not honor him
as God or give thanks to him, but they became futile in
their thinking, and their foolish hearts were darkened.

ROMANS 1:21 ESV

In his letter to Roman believers, the apostle Paul gave a frightening warning. People who knew God stopped honoring Him as God and stopped giving thanks to Him. As a result, their thinking became futile and their hearts were darkened.

Futility, foolishness, and darkness come when people don't esteem and honor the Lord for who He is. He is the Beginning and the End. He is the Creator of all. As the Ancient of Days, all things hold together in Him.

This great, great God makes Himself available to humans. You can know Him. You can and should worship Him and thank Him for all He's done in your life. If you're overwhelmed by the way the world around you ignores and insults the God of the universe, pray for a revival. Pray for your heart to be turned toward Him—and for others to come to know Him as well.

Father, please forgive me for the times I've turned away
from You to chase my own desires. Please forgive me when
I haven't honored You as Lord of all. Thank You for second
chances. Thank You for Your mercy, grace, and forgiveness
that I don't deserve but You so graciously offer.

FACING YOUR FAULTS

*Why should the living complain when punished
for their sins? Let us examine our ways and
test them, and let us return to the LORD.*
LAMENTATIONS 3:39–40 NIV

It's not always easy or enjoyable to consider your weaknesses and flaws. While some people are ultracritical of themselves, for others it's difficult for them to see what they're doing wrong and to decide how to change effectively.

The thing is, if you don't examine your own weaknesses and sins, eventually they'll be discovered. In fact, the Lord disciplines people for their sins; He disciplines His followers as a father disciplines his beloved children.

If you feel like you're facing discipline for your sins, it's time to examine your life and repent. Examine your ways. What are your habits and tendencies? What do you regularly do? Without making any excuses for yourself, come to the Lord and own up to your shortcomings. Ask for forgiveness and choose to change your ways. Return to the Lord in repentance and see how He'll bless you and your penitent heart.

---

*Father, I am sorry. I've sinned against You. I've gone
astray and want to return to You. Please forgive me!*

SUFFERING'S SILVER LINING

*Therefore let those who suffer according
to God's will entrust their souls to a
faithful Creator while doing good.*

1 PETER 4:19 ESV

Suffering is part of life. And as hard as it might be to comprehend or accept, God uses suffering as part of His will. As uncomfortable or as inconvenient as it might seem, suffering can bring about some very positive results—and that's how it can be used as part of the Lord's plan.

If you're in the middle of a season of suffering right now, keep doing good. Don't let your trials distract you from continuing to be a witness for Christ. As you keep doing good even in the middle of hard times, entrust your soul to your Creator. Trust that He is faithful. Trust that He has a good plan He's working out. Sometimes you need to endure suffering in order to come out stronger or to move on to an opportunity you'd never pursue if life were easy.

---

*Father, I don't understand why I have to suffer,
but I know it's under Your watchful eye. I trust
You to protect me and to shower me with Your
mercy as I suffer according to Your will.*

THE GIFT OF HELPING OTHERS

*Do not merely look out for your own personal
interests, but also for the interests of others.*

PHILIPPIANS 2:4 NASB

Selflessly helping other people in the middle of life's ups
and downs can take a lot of your time and energy. It can
add a lot of overwhelm too. You might already feel like
you're up to your eyeballs with your own concerns before
you start helping anyone else.

Yet as demanding as it is to bear someone else's burdens or cheer someone else along, it's a really great gift.
People need your influence in their lives. They need your
care and your listening ear. When you begin to look beyond
your own interests and involve yourself in someone else's
life, it's a blessing. Not only will you help others, but you'll
also be helped as God uses the experiences to shape you
into the woman He wants you to become.

---

*Lord God, please help me overcome my selfish tendency
to only focus on my own concerns. Please open my eyes
to those around me and show me how I can help them. I
want to begin to look out for the interests of others too!*

A HEART AT PEACE

A heart at peace gives life to the body,
but envy rots the bones.
PROVERBS 14:30 NIV

Peace has the power to change everything. You can have a busy life, but if your heart is at peace, you're not overcome with stress. Trials can surprise you on any given day, but if your heart is at peace, you don't get overwhelmed with fear. You might be stunned by bad news yet still be resting with an unexplainable, indescribable peace. Peace gives life to your body and soul. It gives you calm and contentment when the storms of life rage around you.

The absence of peace is a recipe for disaster. Envy will work to rot you from the inside out. Stress will crush you. Worry will consume your thoughts. You can try to drown out a lack of peace with things of this world, but you won't be able to fill the emptiness. True inner peace that comes from God alone will calm and nurture you. True inner peace that comes from God alone will never end.

Father God, thank You for Your true gift
of peace. It's such a life-giving blessing!

WHERE'S YOUR TREASURE?

"Do not store up for yourselves treasures on earth, where moth and rust destroy, and where thieves break in and steal."
MATTHEW 6:19 NASB

Have you ever stopped to consider how much time you spend acquiring and caring for your belongings? When you look at what surrounds you, are you content? Or do you have an insatiable desire for more?

If you've ever noticed how easily your belongings can get ruined—whether you get a stain on your clothes or accidentally break something special or watch the way water or wind or fire damage your home—you know all too well that earthly treasures don't last forever. They're destructible. Without proper upkeep, their worth can plummet in a hurry.

Earthly belongings aren't bad, but they shouldn't become treasures that you quest after with all your time and money.

Father, thank You for my nice belongings. I do like some of them very much for the memories they give me or the way they make me smile. I don't want them to become idols that I treasure, though!

A BETTER TREASURE

"But store up for yourselves treasures in heaven, where neither moth nor rust destroys, and where thieves do not break in or steal, for where your treasure is, there your heart will be also."

MATTHEW 6:20–21 NASB

Since all your earthly belongings are only temporary things that eventually lose value and get ruined, what should you spend your time acquiring? Jesus was very clear in His instruction: instead of storing up treasures on earth, store up treasures in heaven. These heavenly treasures won't perish. They won't get stolen or ruined. They're lasting and worth more than anything here on earth.

Why was Jesus so clear in this teaching? He wanted to help His followers understand how their hearts get tied to whatever they treasure most. If you place great worth in your physical belongings, you'll give part of your heart to those things. But if you realize the worth of your heavenly treasures, your heart will focus on acquiring and caring for those things. Choose the eternal over the temporal. Start focusing on how you can store up treasures in heaven!

Father, please clearly show me what heavenly treasures I've already stored up and how I can begin investing in those lasting, eternal treasures instead of things on this earth.

WHY ARE YOU RESTLESS?

Why are you in despair, my soul? And why are you restless within me? Wait for God, for I will again praise Him for the help of His presence, my God.

PSALM 42:11 NASB

When you feel "off," do you know exactly why? Maybe you woke up in a grumpy mood. Or maybe you're only able to focus on the negative. Do you deal with a restlessness in your soul that you just can't pinpoint?

Knowing that something is wrong inside of you isn't enjoyable, and it's only more aggravating when you have no idea what is wrong. You're not the only one who has felt this way. When the psalmist admitted his soul's despair and restlessness, he couldn't explain what was going on. Even in his confusion, though, he identified the remedy: He needed to wait for God. And he needed to praise Him.

The next time you feel a pang of despair or can't settle the restless feelings inside of you, thank God in advance that through His presence, He'll help you. Then wait for Him to move in your life. Watch the restlessness disappear.

Father, You know me so much better than I know myself. You know why my soul feels like it's in despair. You know why I'm restless. Please help me wait for You. Please help me with Your presence.

DON'T TURN BACK!

But now that you have come to know God, or rather
to be known by God, how can you turn back again to
the weak and worthless elementary principles of the
world, whose slaves you want to be once more?

GALATIANS 4:9 ESV

Every person has a life before Christ. Sadly, those lives often are consumed by pursuing "weak and worthless elementary principles of the world." Without any true freedom, lives without Christ are enslaved to the world. But some people have a life before *and* after Christ. After they realize who Jesus Christ is and what He came to do, the truth of Christ changes their minds and hearts. You can choose to leave the desires of this world behind and trust Him completely. When you come to know God—or, like the apostle Paul clarified, "to be known by God"— keep moving forward in your new life. Forget about your old way of living and press on in your new life of belief. Grow closer to the lover of your soul and you'll put the past behind you.

Lord God, thank You for choosing to know
me. I'm so thankful I have a new life in Christ.
I pray that I would live like it every single day!

TAKING CARE OF YOU

He lets me lie down in green pastures;
He leads me beside quiet waters.

PSALM 23:2 NASB

When Christ becomes your Lord and saves you from the overwhelming weight and punishment of your sin, you begin a new life in Him. He shepherds you in a gentle, but direct, way so you're not left wandering on your own anymore.

The way Christ shepherds His followers is remarkable. He's protective and searches out the best ways to nourish you physically and spiritually. With the Lord as your shepherd, you'll want for nothing. He'll restore your soul and lead you along right paths beside quiet, still waters. You won't need to worry about braving raging seas or tolerating stagnant cesspools—He will lovingly and carefully guide you. But you have to follow Him!

With Christ as your shepherd, you can leave your worries and concerns behind. You don't have to live in fear or confusion. You don't have to feel consumed by overwhelm. You can trust that He'll mercifully lead you in a very good way.

Lord Jesus, I am so thankful You are my good,
good shepherd! Thank You for leading and
guiding me along wonderful pathways. It's
such a relief to trust You and Your loving care.

LOVE

*"I am giving you a new commandment, that you love
one another; just as I have loved you, that you also
love one another. By this all people will know that you
are My disciples: if you have love for one another."*

JOHN 13:34–35 NASB

It's tempting to think you need to step in to solve everyone's problems. Many women like to help. All of that pressure to help other people, though, can start to build up until you feel overwhelmed.

The fascinating realization is that Jesus never asked you to fix everyone. He didn't ask you to get involved in everyone's issues and solve everything. What did He command? He wanted you to love others. Since He was known for His outrageous, extravagant love, He wanted His followers to be known by their love too.

Instead of trying to save the day, switch your focus to showing love with your words and actions. Love others well, and you'll mirror Christ to this overwhelmed world.

---

*Lord Jesus, I want to be like You! Please help
me love others so radically like You did.*

REGAINING CONTROL

Commit to the LORD whatever you do,
and he will establish your plans.
PROVERBS 16:3 NIV

Sometimes in life, tasks and chores get away from you. You know what you need to do. You know what you want to do. But when it comes time to follow through, you don't. And once you start to get behind, it's difficult to regain control.

Instead of giving up in overwhelm and feeling like you can never get back to normal, make a decision. Just like Proverbs says, "Commit to the Lord whatever you do." That includes anything that seems to have fallen behind. In any of your home chores or work tasks or absolutely anything else, commit the work to Him. As you do, pray for guidance. Pray for inspiration and help. Pray for Him to miraculously multiply your time and energy. Then watch the interesting, unexpected ways He will establish your plans.

Father God, I love that You are in control of all things. I don't have to feel overwhelmed by not knowing what to do. You'll help me! I commit to You the tasks we both know I need to accomplish.

SHOWING YOUR LOVE

Dear children, let us not love with words or speech but with actions and in truth.

1 JOHN 3:18 NIV

It's pretty easy to tell someone you love them. In fact, in today's culture, it's typical to say you love a lot of things. Do you love the ocean or mountains? Do you love having a morning cup of coffee? Do you love ice cream or spending time with your friends?

It's so easy to declare your love for a person, place, or thing; but actually acting on your professed love is a whole different story. As the apostle John specified, you can stop loving with your words. Instead, start loving through your actions! Start loving in truth. Let your love be evident to all in the things you say and do. So, without this being just one more item on your to-do list, step out and do something. Instead of only being well intentioned, show your love through your actions.

Father, I know love's not a competition. I don't need to do a huge list of things to prove my love. But I do need to love with more than my words. Please inspire me with powerful ways I can show my love to others.

PERSPECTIVE SHIFT

Set your minds on things that are above,
not on things that are on earth.
COLOSSIANS 3:2 ESV

So much in this world catches your attention and distracts you from what truly matters. The distractions might be urgent, like health concerns. They might be practical, like daily chores. Or they might be frivolous, like fast food or shopping or traveling for enjoyment.

Whatever it is that grabs your attention, keep in mind that it's a distraction from what is truly important. As the apostle Paul taught the Colossian church, believers need to set their minds on things that are above. It's pretty common, though, for your mind to focus on things that are on earth.

On a typical day, is it easy to keep a heavenly perspective? Not always. A lasting, godly train of thought might not seem usual, but it's not impossible. By redirecting your thoughts throughout the day, you can learn how to set your mind on specific thoughts. So work on focusing on eternal things—things that are above.

Father God, I admit I get distracted easily. And I admit I think about things of this world a lot. Deep down, I know they don't matter. Please help me learn to identify them as distractions and shift my attention to You and Your ways.

PREVENTING THE
SNOWBALL EFFECT

Refrain from anger and turn from wrath;
do not fret—it leads only to evil.
PSALM 37:8 NIV

A lot of feelings typically accompany overwhelm—and not many of them are positive. Along with the stress of feeling overwhelmed comes the emotional strain of fretting. Depending on your personality, all the fretting can lead to annoyance, upset, and anger. If you're not careful, your anger can become like a snowball and roll into a huge collection of indignation, vengeance, and wrath.

The potential outcomes from worry and holding on to anger are pretty ugly. Aside from being off-putting to people, they're displeasing to God too. To keep yourself from sin, learn now how to deal with the emotions that come along with your overwhelm. What do you need to prevent? What do you need to change?

Lord, I come to You humbled. Please help me deal with my anxious and angry thoughts before they turn into something much bigger or uglier. I want to glorify You with my attitudes and with the things I say and do.

GOTTA SERVE SOMEBODY

"No one can serve two masters. Either you will hate the one and love the other, or you will be devoted to the one and despise the other. You cannot serve both God and money."

MATTHEW 6:24 NIV

In his song "Gotta Serve Somebody," folk singer Bob Dylan's lyrics reflect biblical truth. Everyone, in fact, does serve somebody or something. The question is who or what you are choosing to serve. Who or what do you consider your master?

As Jesus taught in Matthew, you can't serve both God and money. If you find yourself on a quest for possessions or financial security, money might become your master.

If you're uncertain who or what your master might be but you know you'd like it to be the Lord, make that choice today. Start serving the Lord as your Master. Love and be devoted to Him alone.

Father, I devote myself to You and Your service. Help me turn away from anything else that threatens to come before my love and devotion to You.

ARMED AND READY

Put on the full armor of God, so that you will be able
to stand firm against the schemes of the devil.
EPHESIANS 6:11 NASB

Lots of aspects of everyday life contribute to overwhelm. But there's another aspect that's not often recognized: the schemes of the devil. If you're a believer of Christ, you have an enemy that lurks around, just waiting for the perfect chance to devour you. How does he try to trip you up? With plenty of devious schemes.

Fortunately, you're not left helplessly on your own. The full armor of God will help you stand firm against these schemes. And what is this armor? Paul detailed the armor in Ephesians chapter 6: "Stand firm then, with the belt of truth buckled around your waist, with the breastplate of righteousness in place, and with your feet fitted with the readiness that comes from the gospel of peace. In addition to all this, take up the shield of faith, with which you can extinguish all the flaming arrows of the evil one. Take the helmet of salvation and the sword of the Spirit, which is the word of God" (vv. 14–17 NIV). When you put on this full armor that the Lord provides, you'll be able to stand firm.

Father, thank You for preparing me for battle
by providing so much valuable armor. Help me
stand firm against the schemes of the devil!

NEVER FAILING

How priceless is your unfailing love, O God!
People take refuge in the shadow of your wings.

PSALM 36:7 NIV

Experiencing failure is one sure way to face disappointment and other overwhelming feelings. No one likes to fail, and it's never pleasant when you're counting on something or someone and nothing happens like you expect or hope.

In a world filled with disappointment and failure, it's hard to imagine something that's actually unfailing. We're not used to people or things that are certain, fool-proof, completely dependable or reliable. We're not used to perfection.

Yet the Lord never fails. He is perfect. And His love for you is unfailing. That kind of love and dependability is priceless. Since you can count on it, you can take refuge in Him. He's your protector and provider. He will never ever fail you. Heaven and earth may fall away, but He never will.

Father, Your unfailing love is priceless. It's worth so much more than I'll ever know. I stand in awe that You will never fail me. You're trustworthy. And Your love will endure forever. I praise You for such goodness!

FREEDOM!

It is for freedom that Christ has set us free.
Stand firm, then, and do not let yourselves
be burdened again by a yoke of slavery.

GALATIANS 5:1 NIV

When you enter into a relationship with Christ, there's something special He gives you: true freedom. No matter what happens in this world, no matter who or what tries to hold you back or control you, you are free in Christ. You're not a slave to this world. You're not a slave to addictions. You're not a slave to a person. You are truly free.

As a free woman, what should you do? The best thing to do is live and act and talk like you're free. This still means that you respect your earthly bosses or authorities, but you can live with the freedom that you're not held captive by anything in this world anymore. Instead of living like a caged bird, live like one set free to fly. Break the shackles of overwhelming expectations and choose a life of freedom in Christ.

Lord Jesus, it's a beautiful thing that You chose to set me free just for the sake of freedom. Please help me stand firm in my freedom! I don't want to be burdened any longer.

MY TRUST

In you, LORD my God, I put my trust. I trust in you; do not let me be put to shame, nor let my enemies triumph over me. No one who hopes in you will ever be put to shame, but shame will come on those who are treacherous without cause.

PSALM 25:1–3 NIV

If you tend to trust in yourself, at some point you've wrestled with self-doubt and uncertainty. There's a lot of pressure involved in deciding the best thing to do.

When you change from trusting in yourself to trusting in the Lord, though, that doubt is gone. Of course you're not sure what will happen in your future, but no one is. What you can rest in is the fact that the Lord has your best interests at heart. No matter what happens to you, He'll work it all for good when you love Him. He's a trustworthy God. Take it from King David: no one who hopes in the Lord will ever be put to shame. David knew the Lord his God was and is trustworthy. And you can know it too.

In You, Lord my God, I put my trust. Forgive me for all the times I've tried to trust in myself. Please help me surrender myself fully to You.

PHYSICAL AND SPIRITUAL THERAPY

Therefore lift your drooping hands and strengthen your weak knees, and make straight paths for your feet, so that what is lame may not be put out of joint but rather be healed.
HEBREWS 12:12–13 ESV

If you've ever experienced physical therapy, you know it takes a lot of hard work and pain to heal and restore certain body parts and functions. Health issues and rehabilitation are no joke—they take a lot of intense effort, repetition, and endurance.

Just like physical therapy takes time, effort, and energy, spiritual therapy does too. What is spiritual therapy? Just like physical therapy involves singling out certain body parts and strategically exercising them to make them stronger, spiritual therapy involves figuring out some of your weaknesses and exercising them.

If you wish you could improve your prayer life but you think it will only ever be a wish, it's time to start praying! If obedience to the Lord tends to be a weakness, it's time to practice obeying instead of caving in to your sin nature. Practice the spiritual disciplines you've always wanted to be a normal part of your life.

Father, I want my faith in You to grow stronger! Please help me exercise and strengthen my spiritual muscles. I'm ready and willing to grow closer to You so I can be used by You!

KNOWLEDGE AND UNDERSTANDING

The one who has knowledge uses words with restraint,
and whoever has understanding is even-tempered.

PROVERBS 17:27 NIV

Would you like to be known as a woman who's knowledgeable and understanding? Or would you like people to consider you to be a woman who's ignorant and thoughtless?

The Bible clearly describes how you can achieve either lifestyle. Since the woman of wisdom, knowledge, and understanding seems more desirable, how can that kind of life be achieved?

Proverbs reveals that a knowledgeable woman will use her words with restraint. So instead of letting any thought fly out of your mouth, think and consider before you speak. Proverbs also reveals that a woman of understanding has an even temper. If you have a tendency to fly off the handle in anger and rage, you'll need to increase your understanding.

By choosing restraint instead of liberty and independence, you'll show yourself to be wise, knowledgeable, and understanding.

Father, I do want to become a woman of knowledge
and understanding. Please help me stop
and think before I say and do!

DEALING WITH ANXIETY?

Cast all your anxiety on him because he cares for you.
1 PETER 5:7 NIV

Do you regularly take on the heavy weight that comes with worrying about all that might possibly happen? When you're worn down by apprehension and anxiety, you might wish you could break free. But how can you find freedom? How can you feel at peace?

The apostle Peter shared one effective way to still your mental strife: Give all your cares to the Lord. Cast all your anxieties on Him. Throw all your concerns on His shoulders. Then, once you leave your worries with Him, you can relax.

Take a big sigh of relief, because He cares for you. He watches over you attentively and affectionately. Turn in all your overwhelming fears, and then let Him overwhelm you with His deep love and unexplainable peace.

Father, I surrender all my cares and concerns to You!
Thank You for caring about me so deeply. Thank
You for offering freedom and peace of mind.

YOU ARE WHAT YOU THINK

Finally, brothers and sisters, whatever is true, whatever is honorable, whatever is right, whatever is pure, whatever is lovely, whatever is commendable, if there is any excellence and if anything worthy of praise, think about these things.

PHILIPPIANS 4:8 NASB

What you think about usually determines what you become. So to help shape and direct your life in a positive way, think in a positive way.

In his letter to Philippian believers, the apostle Paul summed up what things need to consume believers' thoughts. Think about what's true. Think about whatever is honorable. Think about what's right. Think about what's pure. Think about what's lovely. Think about what's worth commending. Think about excellent things. Think about anything worthy of praise.

As you fix your thoughts on those true, honorable, right, pure, lovely, commendable, excellent, praiseworthy things, they'll influence your attitude and your life. You'll begin to become what you think.

Father, I really would love to become a true, honorable, right, pure, lovely woman. Please help me zero in on commendable, excellent, and praiseworthy thoughts. Help me transform my life through my right thinking.

MY TIMES ARE IN YOUR HAND

But I trust in you, O Lord; I say, "You are my God."
My times are in your hand; rescue me from the
hand of my enemies and from my persecutors!

PSALM 31:14–15 ESV

It's an incredibly beautiful thing to reach the point in your faith where you trust in the Lord so much to say, "My times are in Your hand." This is the point of surrender when you know you trust Him completely. And this is the point where you'll experience the most peace.

Knowing with absolute certainty that the Lord is your God is powerful. Your fear disappears. Your concern about details fades, because you know who is in control. You can trust that your heavenly Father cares for you and has a plan for your life. He can rescue you from your enemies and persecutors.

Know that your times are in His hand. He's chosen to place you in this very spot of history for a reason. Trust Him to use you for such a time as this!

Lord, You are my God. I trust in You! I'm so thankful I can rest in the fact that my times are in Your hand. Please lead and direct me in a very clear way. I love You!

NO WORRIES!

"For this reason I say to you, do not be worried about your life, as to what you will eat or what you will drink; nor for your body, as to what you will put on. Is life not more than food, and the body more than clothing?"

MATTHEW 6:25 NASB

Are you a worrier by nature? Have you ever worn your worries proudly like a badge of honor? People can mull over possibilities until they turn into obsessions. Some situations in life merit concern. But others? Some things just aren't worth worrying about. So many times, worries are just potential situations that most likely will never happen.

Jesus clearly taught that you don't have to be worried about your life. The Lord knows and loves you so very much. He's promised to take care of you. He knows exactly what you need even before you do. Because of this, if you have a tendency to worry, give your worries to Him. Remind yourself that He's promised to provide basic necessities like your food and clothing. He's promised not to withhold any good thing from those who walk uprightly. Instead of spending your time worrying, spend your time living a right life in the Lord's eyes!

Father, because of You, I have no need to worry. When concerns flood my brain and I'm tempted to panic, please fill me with Your peace. I want to remember that You are my strength and my shield.

WORRY'S ACHIEVEMENTS

"Can any one of you by worrying
add a single hour to your life?"
MATTHEW 6:27 NIV

Do you know what you can achieve by worrying? Worrying will give you plenty of side effects—like difficulties concentrating, difficulties making decisions, disrupted sleep, elevated levels of the stress hormone cortisol, exhaustion, headaches, irritability, nausea, and tense muscles. But even with all those physical and mental effects that come along with worry, you won't actually achieve anything.

At some point in life, you'll need to come to terms with the fact that certain things are out of your control. In fact, many things are out of your control. From other people to world events to exactly when you'll die, you have no control. In today's control-freak era where everyone wants to have a say about everything, this truth can be hard to swallow.

Instead of bemoaning the fact that so much is out of your control, start praising the Lord who *is* in control of everything. Trust Him and seek His will. While you won't be able to add a single hour to your life, you'll be able to add to the quality of your life.

Father, I trust You! Thank You that I don't have to worry
about a thing. Truly, You've got everything under control.

FASHION SHOW

*"And why are you worried about clothing? Notice how the
lilies of the field grow; they do not labor nor do they spin
thread for cloth, yet I say to you that not even Solomon
in all his glory clothed himself like one of these."*

MATTHEW 6:28–29 NASB

Everyone needs to wear clothing. And different occasions
call for different outfit choices. You wouldn't wear the same
outfit for working outside that you would to a wedding.

Even though clothing is a necessity, Jesus taught that
you don't need to be consumed with thinking about it.
Even King Solomon, the richest man, didn't wear clothing
as spectacular as the way the Lord clothes the lilies. Since
God naturally provides stunning beauty for living things, of
course He has the ability and resources to clothe you too.

Looking to the Lord for your clothing can seem a bit
strange until you invite Him into the process. The next
time you're ready to shop for clothes, pray first. Pray for
Him to provide what you need. Pray for Him to open
your eyes to what you should purchase. Then patiently
wait for Him to surprise you with opportunities. He
really will clothe you like the lilies of the field.

*Father, thank You for taking care of my needs and
so many of my wants. I want to learn to bring
You all of my life, even my shopping habits.*

KNOWING YOUR NECESSITIES

*"So do not worry, saying, 'What shall we eat?' or
'What shall we drink?' or 'What shall we wear?'
For the pagans run after all these things, and your
heavenly Father knows that you need them."*

MATTHEW 6:31–32 NIV

Depending on your circumstances, you may be genuinely concerned about how you'll afford groceries or what you have to wear. When you're not sure exactly how you'll be able to pay for basic necessities, Jesus' teaching seems out of touch.

When Jesus made the distinction between the way the pagans worry and run after necessities, He was addressing a heart matter or a trust issue. Jesus knew pagans trusted in themselves to provide food and clothing, with no regard to the Lord.

Since believers are known and loved by their heavenly Father, He will provide for them. Just as earthly fathers give good gifts to their children, won't your heavenly Father do so much more for you? If you're truly concerned about your necessities, take those requests to the Lord in prayer. Ask Him to multiply your money or help you find just what you need. You may end up being very surprised by the way He provides!

---

*Father, I'm thankful I can trust You for absolutely everything,
even my food and clothing. Please help me not worry about
the way You'll provide. I'd rather trust You completely!*

FOCUSING ON TODAY

"So do not worry about tomorrow;
for tomorrow will worry about itself.
Each day has enough trouble of its own."
MATTHEW 6:34 NASB

In this fear-driven culture, so many potential concerns are splashed across news headlines. What if the absolute worst-case scenario happens? Many of those headlines hint that if only you could take dozens of precautions, maybe you could make a difference.

But what if the fear-based propaganda only spreads worries? What if you didn't need to worry about tomorrow? All throughout history, people have had many valid reasons to be concerned. Because we live in a fallen world, there's no perfection outside of eternity.

Still, Jesus taught that you don't have to worry about tomorrow. Each day has enough trouble of its own. If you tend to get really upset by worrying about future possibilities, try just focusing on today. What is required of you today? What needs your attention? When you feel worries and what-ifs start to creep in, take them to the Lord in prayer. Surrender those concerns to Him, and go about your day doing the good work He's called you to do.

Father, I choose to live by faith in You and not by fear that's encouraged by the world. Please help me focus on Your truth instead of all that might or might not happen.

NONCONFORMITY

*Do not conform to the pattern of this world, but be
transformed by the renewing of your mind. Then
you will be able to test and approve what God's
will is—his good, pleasing and perfect will.*

ROMANS 12:2 NIV

The world doesn't always look kindly on nonconformists.
Often considered free spirits, individualists, loners, and
mavericks, nonconformists don't adhere to a generally
accepted thought or action.

Yet isn't that the call of a believer? Followers of Christ
shouldn't conform to the world's patterns. Instead of
following the crowd, a believer chooses to test and weigh
everything against God's Word and His will. As you
discern what would glorify and please God, you'll make
right choices that may or may not look like the world's
trending patterns.

*Lord God, thank You for Your good, pleasing,
and perfect will. I would rather follow You and
Your ways than the ways of the world. Please give
me discernment to know the difference between Your
good, right ways and the world's evil, wrong ways.*

A GOOD NIGHT OF SLEEP

*The fear of the LORD leads to life, so that one
may sleep satisfied, untouched by evil.*

PROVERBS 19:23 NASB

If you've ever been plagued by sleepless nights, you know
that a good night's sleep is a gift. There's something so
refreshing and restorative in sleeping soundly all night long.
Sometimes you can't help it if your environment disrupts
your sleep. Sometimes your own thoughts can keep you
awake for most of the night. And other times, you wake
up—and stay awake—for no known reason.

The book of Proverbs offers great advice for a good
night of sleep: fear the Lord. When you regard the Lord
with honor, respect, and a healthy dose of fear, you'll
experience life and peace. That life and peace will bring
so much satisfaction that even your sleep will be blessed.

---

*My God and Savior, I do honor You as Lord of all!
Awed by Your power and majesty, I come to You
in fear. Thank You for working in my life in such a
way that even my sleep is better because of You.*

FEAR FACTOR

*There is no fear in love, but perfect love drives
out fear, because fear involves punishment, and
the one who fears is not perfected in love.*

1 JOHN 4:18 NASB

Fear is a menace that robs you of joy and steals your peace. Fear fills you with alarm, leaving you feeling on edge because of the way you anticipate danger or misfortune. Yet fear isn't always justified. Sometimes fears are completely unfounded. Sometimes they multiply like weeds, taking root in your mind until they spread uncontrollably.

If you're weary of always feeling apprehensive and anxious, it's time to examine your heart and mind. How can you drive out fear? How can you break free from the chains of fear that enslave you? The apostle John's advice is to be perfected in love. There is no fear in love. In fact, perfect love drives out fear.

The big question is whether you're experiencing love. Do you know the eternal love of Christ? It won't shift and change like love shown by humans. It's sacrificial, lasting, and powerful. In fact, it has the capability to banish your fear.

The next time you notice fear creeping into your thoughts and feelings, stop and consider God's love for you. He loved you so much He sent His only Son to become a sacrifice so you could have life forever. That's the best, most confident assurance possible.

---

*Lord Jesus, thank You for Your love and
the way it casts out all fear in me.*

REJOICE!

Rejoice in the Lord always. I will say it again: Rejoice!
PHILIPPIANS 4:4 NIV

In the face of overwhelm, there's one powerful defense that might seem unusual. Rejoice!

This rejoicing might seem ludicrous in the middle of a crisis. When you feel so overwhelmed it's hard to breathe, rejoicing may be the last thing on your mind. But rejoice anyway. Find joy. Find a reason to praise God and do it! Rejoice in the opportunities He's placed before you. Rejoice for whatever season of life you're entering or leaving. Rejoice for all the good gifts He brings to you each and every day. Rejoice!

As you rejoice, your attention will turn to what's so very good in your life. When you choose to rejoice, you'll focus on your Maker and how very good He is. Rejoicing will add spring to your step and appreciation to your mind. "Rejoice in the Lord always. I will say it again: Rejoice!"

---

*Lord, I rejoice in You! Thank You for always
giving me some reason to be joyful.*

SUSTAINED

*I lay down and slept; I woke again, for the L<small>ORD</small> sustained
me. I will not be afraid of many thousands of people
who have set themselves against me all around.*

<small>PSALM 3:5–6 ESV</small>

When David feared for his life, he had plenty of valid
reasons. He didn't just imagine his enemies were out to
get him. Seriously wanting to kill him, they sought him
on an all-out manhunt. The amazing thing is that even
though thousands joined his son Absalom and set themselves against David, they never caught him.

What's even more amazing? In the middle of all the
overwhelming turmoil, David could actually lie down
and sleep. Sleep! He could sleep and not be discovered,
because the Lord sustained him.

If you're in the middle of a miserable trial where you
feel like all hope is gone, don't despair. The Lord loves you
and has a plan for you. He will sustain you. Put your trust
in Him and choose not to be afraid, even if thousands of
people set themselves against you.

---

*Lord, thank You for sustaining those You love!
Because of You, I have absolutely nothing to fear.*

STAND

Therefore put on the full armor of God, so that when the day of evil comes, you may be able to stand your ground, and after you have done everything, to stand.

EPHESIANS 6:13 NIV

Have you ever considered that when God blesses your work and you're pursuing and serving Him, your enemy ramps up his battle? That might sound daunting, especially if you think your service to God should be problem-free.

What should you do when the day of evil comes and you need to be prepared to battle? First, you need to put on the full armor of God—and that includes equipping yourself with truth, righteousness, the Gospel of peace, faith, salvation, and the Word of God.

Once you've equipped yourself, the next step is to stand firm. This standing firm involves holding your ground by standing against your enemy in resistance. As you stand firm, the Lord will fight for you. Don't give up!

Father God, thank You for Your full armor! It's such a relief to know I don't have to battle against Satan completely on my own. You equip me in a marvelous way. I want to stand my ground against the enemy's attacks. Please help me hold my ground as You fight my battles.

WHOM SHALL YOU FEAR?

*"Do not be afraid of those who kill the body but
cannot kill the soul. Rather, be afraid of the One
who can destroy both soul and body in hell."*

MATTHEW 10:28 NIV

Do you regularly live in fear of people around you? Are
you concerned about what others think or how you might
be treated? Do certain groups in this world fill you with
fear and dread? Do you get scared when you imagine the
future? Depending on your answers, you may need to make
some changes in your life.

What would your life look like if you chose to walk
away from that fear? What if you had no fear of *anything*
in this world? What if you didn't fear a single person or
entity? What if no potential situation struck fear in your
heart? . . .

What would your life look like if the only One you
feared was God? As Jesus said, don't be afraid of people.
Be afraid of the Lord Almighty. After all, He is the One
who can destroy both soul and body in hell. And He is
the One to graciously save all those who worship and
trust in Him.

---

*Father God, please help me forget my fear of people
and situations. Help me live with honor and
reverence for You, my light and salvation.*

GROANING

I am feeble and utterly crushed;
I groan in anguish of heart.

PSALM 38:8 NIV

When you're feeble, you feel it. Deep down, you know you simply can't muster the strength you need. You might feel physically feeble and be fully aware of your limitations and lack of abilities. Or you might be mentally or spiritually feeble and feel like life has taken a huge, crushing toll on you.

When feebleness crashes in with crushing blows, it's okay to lament. When your heart feels utterly anguished, it's okay to groan. Cry out to the Lord your God with honesty. Grieve. Tell Him every single feeling you're experiencing. Cry out for mercy. Ask Him for His divine help and deliverance. Bare your soul to your heavenly Father, then wait in expectation for His comfort and love. Choose to walk through this time of despair and disappointment with the lover of your soul.

Lord God, help me! Please restore my strength.
I cling to You alone as I feel feeble and
crushed in the midst of my anguish.

KEEP ON!

Let's not become discouraged in doing good, for in due time we will reap, if we do not become weary.
GALATIANS 6:9 NASB

Weariness is such a frustrating, exhausting state. Whenever you reach the point of wearing out with tiredness, it can be discouraging. You might wonder if there's a reason to keep doing good. Why keep doing everything you've been doing if all it does is wear you out?

There's nothing new about weariness. The apostle Paul addressed the issue with Galatian believers centuries ago. And although knowing that weariness is a universal feeling doesn't make it easier to navigate or experience, Paul did give some advice for believers: keep doing good!

Even if you think you're reaching the point of exhaustion, keep on keeping on. Look to the Lord for your strength and don't let discouragement get you down. Choose to keep doing good, with the promise that eventually you'll reap what you sow. If you keep planting seeds of goodness now, all that goodness will grow into a bumper crop that will leave you feeling so thankful you never gave up.

Father, I'm tired. I feel a deep weariness. I don't want to quit, though. Please give me the strength and energy and desire to keep doing good.

REST AND WAIT

*Rest in the LORD and wait patiently for Him; do not
get upset because of one who is successful in his way,
because of the person who carries out wicked schemes.*

PSALM 37:7 NASB

If you tend to pay attention to other people around you,
it's really tempting and easy to give jealousy and envy a
foothold. Social media is a notorious mental battleground,
as it's filled with images of others smiling and living what
appear to be perfect lives.

Your life certainly doesn't feel perfect; you're more than
aware of your shortcomings and all that you're lacking.
Your life doesn't look perfect either, because you know the
messy parts that drive you up the wall.

Instead of comparing yourself to others, choose to stop.
Don't get upset when you see others succeeding, even if
it seems like they're going about their successes in a less-
than-savory way. Choose to wait patiently for the Lord.
Even if He takes so much longer than you'd ever imagine,
rest in Him. Wait on Him and His timing. Then rejoice
when He works in an amazing way in His amazing time.

---

*Lord, I choose to wait patiently for You! As I wait,
please help me truly rest in You. Thank
You for filling me with Your peace.*

PEACE UNLIKE ANYTHING ELSE

"Peace I leave with you; my peace I give to you. Not as the world gives do I give to you. Let not your hearts be troubled, neither let them be afraid."

JOHN 14:27 ESV

Peace is such a huge gift that comforts and fulfills like nothing else. But you can't go out and buy peace when you're running low. You can't ask for it as a birthday gift and wait for its delivery.

True peace comes from Christ alone. He came into the world to bring peace. And when you come to trust Him as your Lord and Savior, He fills your heart and your life with an inexplicable peace. His peace can't be explained or even fully understood. But you can experience it. His peace will remove your fear and any trouble in your heart of hearts. His peace will fill your soul with a beautiful tranquility that's unlike anything else.

Lord Jesus, You gave such a beautiful gift by coming into the world. Thank You for leaving Your peace with everyone who calls on You in love and trust.

A LIFE OF INTEGRITY

The integrity of the upright guides them, but the crookedness of the treacherous destroys them.

PROVERBS 11:3 ESV

What does a life of integrity look like? You might think it's a life characterized by honesty and fairness, but integrity also means being complete, whole, and undivided.

If you want to live a life of integrity, you'll need to choose to stand up for what's right while turning away from all that's wrong and deceptive. To picture this kind of life, it might be helpful to imagine two trees. One has a trunk that's completely straight like a column. The other has a crooked trunk that bends this way and that. They're both trees, but if they were planted side by side, you'd see a noticeable difference.

A life of integrity is like that upright tree, and a treacherous life is like the crooked one. Filled with deception, sinful choices, and dishonest gain, the treacherous betray your trust. And all those unreliable inconsistencies will end up destroying the treacherous.

Even if it seems uncomfortable to live an upright, honest life, do it. Your integrity will be worth it in the long run.

Father, please help me glorify You and point others to You by choosing and living a life of integrity.

TAKE HEART

And after you have suffered a little while, the God of
all grace, who has called you to his eternal glory in Christ,
will himself restore, confirm, strengthen, and establish you.

1 PETER 5:10 ESV

When you're in the middle of suffering, it often feels like it will never end. Just like being stuck in a dark place, you can't spy even a glimmer of light at the end of your tunnel of suffering.

Yet your suffering won't last forever. If you face death, your suffering will end. For believers of Christ, that death will be transformed into eternal glory.

If you feel overwhelmed by suffering right now, what can you anticipate? The apostle Peter shared that the God of all grace will Himself restore you. That means He'll give back something that's been taken from you. He'll confirm you and make you more certain than ever. He'll make you stronger. And if all that's not enough, He'll establish you too, by creating something or placing you in a position that will last for a very long time.

Take heart! The God of all grace will work good in the middle of your suffering!

Father God, I trust You completely. In my suffering,
I surrender myself to You. Please will and
work in Your very good way.

SHINE BRIGHT

Do everything without grumbling or arguing,
so that you may become blameless and pure,
children of God without fault in a warped and crooked
generation. Then you will shine among them like stars
in the sky as you hold firmly to the word of life.

PHILIPPIANS 2:14–16 NIV

If you've spent much time with a grumbler, you know all too well the frustration you experience when all you hear is complaint after complaint.

Instead of complaining or arguing with others, pick a different approach to life. If you tend to have a negative personality, you may need to be more diligent in choosing positivity. Decide to find and focus on any hint of good. As you choose to stop yourself from grumbling or arguing, you'll be noticeably different in this world. Shining like a bright star in this dark, dark world, your kindness and blameless purity will stand out. Choose to shine the light of Christ through your words and attitudes!

Father, please change my attitude! I don't want to find
fault in so much. I don't want to grumble or complain, and
I don't want to argue with others. Please help me shine
Christ's light in this dark world by the things I say and do.

WHERE IS HE?

Why, LORD, do you stand far off? Why do
you hide yourself in times of trouble?
PSALM 10:1 NIV

When you're living through the worst time of your life, you might wonder where the Lord is. It feels like He's standing far off as you face things you never dreamed of facing. It feels like He's hiding just when you need Him most. When you cry out to Him, it doesn't feel like your prayers make a bit of difference.

Where is the Lord? When will He come to your aid?

When you feel like you're all alone and wonder when He'll come to your rescue, remind yourself of His character. Search the scriptures for what you know is true about Him. Then remind yourself of His promises. He's promised to never leave nor forsake you. He's promised to renew your strength. He's promised that all things will work together for your good. Keep trusting in Him and His promises. Wait for His help. He will sustain you when you need Him most.

Lord Almighty, where are You? I'm praying to
You from such a place of despair and pain.
Please help me. I need You, my Father!

SOLID AS A ROCK

"Everyone then who hears these words of mine and does them will be like a wise man who built his house on the rock. And the rain fell, and the floods came, and the winds blew and beat on that house, but it did not fall, because it had been founded on the rock."

MATTHEW 7:24–25 ESV

Have you ever taken the time to read Jesus' words? The New Testament books of Matthew, Mark, Luke, and John are filled with them. When you do read them, you'll notice that Jesus' commands and teachings are direct. What does Jesus ask you to do? How does He ask you to act?

When you choose to obey Christ and all He taught, you begin to build a very firm foundation for your faith and your life. Just like building a house on a strong rock, your life's foundation will be established on the strong rock of Christ. When the storms of life blow, you won't be destroyed. Obedience to Christ's commands will form the foundation of your faith. It's time to get building!

Lord Jesus, I want to know You and what You've asked of Your followers. I want to obey Your commands and build a strong foundation for my life.

DO OR DO NOT

"Everyone who hears these words of mine and does not do them will be like a foolish man who built his house on the sand. And the rain fell, and the floods came, and the winds blew and beat against that house, and it fell, and great was the fall of it."

MATTHEW 7:26–27 ESV

If you've ever watched the Star Wars movies, you may remember Yoda's quote: "Do or do not, there is no try." Wise little Yoda offered fantastic advice that any believer of Christ can follow. As Jesus taught, everyone who hears His words has a choice to make: either do what He says or don't do what He says.

If you hear what Christ commands and choose to ignore Him, you end up being like a foolish man who built his house on sand. When storms came and completely wiped out the man's house, he lost everything. Yet it shouldn't have come as a surprise, because he had chosen a weak, faulty foundation.

As you hear Christ's teachings, decide right away if you'll listen and obey or turn the other way. But keep in mind that your life will absolutely reflect the wisdom or foolishness of your decision.

Lord Jesus, thank You for sharing Your wisdom. Give me strength and courage to do what You ask. I want to build my life on the truth and strength of You!

GIVE ME LIFE

Turn my eyes from looking at worthless
things; and give me life in your ways.
PSALM 119:37 ESV

So much in this world is worthless. Granted, many things bring pleasure and enjoyment, and there's plenty of fun to be had. But out of all these ways to spend your time and money, how many of them have lasting value? How many of them possess worth?

Sometimes it's easy to get caught up in chasing after ways to make yourself feel better, and you gloss over what's truly important. If you know this is a weakness in your life, don't be afraid to confess it to your heavenly Father. He knows your tendencies already, so it's not like it's a big surprise to Him.

Ask Him to help you identify the areas of your life where you gravitate toward worthless things. Then ask Him to turn your eyes away from them. Ask Him to give you life in His ways. As you do, you'll notice a change in your life. Start following His ways more and more and discover truly worthwhile things!

Father, so much of my life is consumed by things that
don't last. I don't want my life to be defined by that.
Please turn my eyes to what's eternally meaningful.
Please shift my perspective and change my heart.

LOVE OTHERS

*For the entire law is fulfilled in keeping this one command:
"Love your neighbor as yourself." If you bite and devour each
other, watch out or you will be destroyed by each other.*

The simple biblical command to love your neighbor as yourself can bring up so many nitpicky points. Some people want to define exactly who their neighbor might be and who their neighbor might not be. Other people try to figure out what it means to love. Still others contemplate how they'd personally like to receive love.

But all of that seems to skirt around the main point: followers of Christ should be known by their love. Followers of Christ need to love others. Plenty of actions and attitudes do the opposite of love. If you have a tendency to devour someone with your words or actions, that's decidedly unloving. If you act in a cruel, destructive way, that's decidedly unloving.

Difficult or not, if you love Christ, you need to love others in all you say and do.

---

*Lord Jesus, I do love You! And I do want to be known by
my love for You and others. Please help me get past my
sin and love others well, whether I feel like it or not.*

ARE YOU IN TROUBLE?

In the day of my trouble I seek the Lord; in the night my hand is stretched out without wearying; my soul refuses to be comforted.

PSALM 77:2 ESV

You'll experience countless troubles in this life. From minor inconveniences to major problems, you never know when something might go wrong. But you don't have to go through life looking for trouble, and you don't have to focus on every single wrong thing that happens.

Instead, when trouble does hit and you don't know what to do, seek the Lord. Ask for His help and guidance. Ask for His relief. Cry out for mercy. Until you see Him at work, keep pleading with Him. Don't grow weary of stretching out your hands in prayer. Don't give up when He seems silent or distant. Refuse to be comforted until the Lord of peace intervenes. Bring your cares and concerns to Him and seek His help.

Abba, Father, help me! I am in trouble and choose to turn to You. I trust You to help me. Please shower me with Your mercy and favor.

OVERCOMING THE WORLD

For everyone who has been born of God overcomes the world. And this is the victory that has overcome the world—our faith. Who is it that overcomes the world except the one who believes that Jesus is the Son of God?

1 JOHN 5:4–5 ESV

So many people believe and act like everything with meaning or purpose is found in this world. Finding their identities in their jobs or status or relationships, they set this world on a pedestal and willingly bow to it with their money, time, and attention.

Yet this world is passing away. Everything that's in it is temporary. It won't last. So when it's promised that those who believe that Jesus is the Son of God will overcome the world, that brings hope. Knowing that faith alone prevails and triumphs over the things of the world brings comfort.

Instead of chasing after all the world holds dear, chase after Jesus. Get to know and love Him. Watch your faith and belief in Him grow. You'll experience a much more meaningful life as a result.

Lord Jesus, I believe You are the Son of God! I'm thankful for my faith in You, and I'm so glad that through You I can overcome the world.

CHOOSING YOUR RESPONSE

*Fools show their annoyance at once,
but the prudent overlook an insult.*

PROVERBS 12:16 NIV

You never know who you might meet or need to deal with in this life. Some people are truly delightful to get to know. Out of deep kindness, they'll go out of their way to bless your life. Other people are downright nasty. Because they're focused on themselves and obsessed with making their own opinions known, you may feel worse for knowing them.

Regardless of who you'll meet, it's important to choose your responses wisely. Fools love to get annoyed and offended, and they'll quickly tell their disgust to anyone who's within earshot. But prudent people overlook insults. They choose to treat others with respect. And, like Christ commanded, they choose to love even the unlovable. That kind of kindness and compassion might not be easy, but it's definitely wise.

What kind of response will you choose today?

---

*Father, I want to be prudent. Even when
I'm wronged or offended, please help me
respond in a gracious, gentle way.*

ALL THINGS

And we know that God causes all things to work
together for good to those who love God, to those
who are called according to His purpose.

ROMANS 8:28 NASB

For believers, one of the most comforting Bible verses may
be Romans 8:28. Knowing that God causes all things to
work together for good is a huge promise.

It's easy to imagine good coming from wonderful
experiences in your life. But when times are tough? Or
downright miserable? It can be hard to believe that any
good can come from extreme suffering. Yet good *can* come
from the worst times of your life; even your pain will work
together for good.

If you love God, you're called according to His purpose. And if you're called according to His purpose, you
can rest in the fact that all things will work together for
good. *All things.*

Father, please take all my brokenness and pain,
all my overwhelm and agony, and cause
it all to work together for good.

WHAT'S YOUR REQUEST?

Do not be anxious about anything, but in everything
by prayer and pleading with thanksgiving let your
requests be made known to God. And the peace
of God, which surpasses all comprehension, will
guard your hearts and minds in Christ Jesus.

PHILIPPIANS 4:6–7 NASB

Do you feel weighed down and overwhelmed by the cares of the world? Upset by current events? Frustrated and disgusted by the blatant sin that's celebrated in this world?

Even with all those legitimate concerns, the apostle Paul reminds you not to be anxious about them. Specifically, he says you should not be anxious about anything.

Instead of anxiety and overwhelm, choose prayer. Tell God about what's weighing on your heart and mind. Thank Him and plead with Him. As you pray and continue to pray, something magnificent will happen: His peace will guard your heart and your mind. Even when you won't be able to comprehend or understand His peace, it will wash over you. When you come to Him with your burdens and requests, His peace will take away your anxieties.

Father God, thank You for Your peace. I can't understand
the way it works, but I know I experience it. The way
it guards my heart and mind is truly amazing.

CRY OUT TO HIM!

*In my distress I called to the LORD; I cried to my
God for help. From his temple he heard my voice;
my cry came before him, into his ears.*

PSALM 18:6 NIV

When you're hurting or scared or so confused or you feel
like you're in distress, don't keep it inside, all bottled up.
Don't be afraid to share what you're really thinking or feeling. Instead of telling anyone who might listen, choose to
tell One in particular. Call to the Lord. Cry to your God.

As you call out and cry to the Lord, He hears your
voice. He knows what you need. He listens to your concerns and cares. You don't have to face your distress all by
yourself. You can involve your heavenly Father, confidently
resting in the truth that He hears, He knows, and He cares
for you. He's your rock, your fortress, and your deliverer.
He's your shield, your salvation, and your stronghold. He
will come to your rescue.

---

*Heavenly Father, thank You for hearing my cries for help!
Thank You for knowing me completely and choosing to
love and save me. You are completely worthy of my trust!*

HIS GOOD GIFT OF PEACE

*Now may the Lord of peace himself give you peace
at all times in every way. The Lord be with you all.*

2 THESSALONIANS 3:16 ESV

Overwhelm enters your life in so many different ways.
From the demands of this world to the demands you
place on yourself, you try to juggle so much every day.
Yet even with all that you find yourself facing, peace can
be yours. You can experience peace in the middle of all
that you need to do.

How can you discover peace in the overwhelm? The
Lord of peace Himself will give you peace at all times
and in every way. You won't be able to create or find this
peace on your own; it's one of His many good gifts He
gives to those He loves. Through the Lord, rest in and
relish every bit of the peace He offers you, because it is
His good, good gift.

---

*Lord of peace, thank You for working in my heart. You've
created me, and You've allowed all circumstances in
my life for a reason. Even when I feel like I'm in over my
head, please work through me. Please grant me Your
good gift of peace in the middle of my overwhelm.*

SCRIPTURE INDEX

OLD TESTAMENT